THE PRACTICE
OF PRAYER

THE PRACTICE OF PRAYER

PSALMS (SELECTED) / HOWARD WALLACE

AN ALBATROSS BOOK

◈ the bible reading fellowship
OPENING THE BIBLE

© Howard Wallace 1993

Published in Australia and New Zealand by
Albatross Books Pty Ltd
PO Box 320, Sutherland
NSW 2232, Australia
in the United States of America by
Albatross Books
PO Box 131, Claremont
CA 91711, USA
and in the United Kingdom by
The Bible Reading Fellowship
Peter's Way, Sandy Lane West
Oxford OX4 5HG, England

First edition 1993

National Library of Australia
Cataloguing-in-Publication data

Wallace, Howard
The Practice of Prayer

ISBN 0 7324 1020 7 (Albatross)
ISBN 0 7459 2439 5 (BRF)

1. Bible. O.T. Psalms–Commentaries.
I. Title

223.207

Cover photo: John Graham
Printed and bound by Griffin Paperbacks, Netley, SA

Contents

To my constant companion,
Bronwyn

Foreword

There is a revival in Psalms study taking place throughout the Western Christian world. This revival has been led to some extent by a renewed interest in the use of the Book of Psalms in the music of the church and in its worship. But this revival has been accompanied by a shift in the focus of scholarly interest in the Psalms.

In the earlier part of this century, most scholars investigating the Book of Psalms were interested in historical questions. That is, they were concerned about the origins of the psalms, how they were composed, and how they were used in the worship of ancient Israel. Much of that has now changed. Interest is focussed more these days on how the psalms relate to the life of the person who uses them as prayers and hymns; or on the whole collection of the Book of Psalms and whether any overall pattern can be seen in it; or on the psalms as pieces of literature and how they can be meaningful for a whole host of people who come from different ages and situations. Revival in interest in the Book of Psalms has been encouraged by the production of a number of new study books over the last two decades. Most of these study books have been intended for non-specialists.

It is a lively time for those who have a scholarly interest in the Psalms or who lead worship. But it should also be a lively time for those of us who read the Psalms in the course of our public worship or private devotions. Fresh insights into how the Psalms can serve us in our worship or in the quest for understanding and meaning in our lives are coming to the fore. A study of the Psalms can present new possibilities and opportunities for the expression of the Christian faith and understanding of God. The Psalms can open up for us new perspectives on the nature of the gospel.

The Psalms have always been part of the Christian tradition. They have been used by various denominations or religious orders in their worship and devotions over the centuries. As we approach the twenty-first century, there is opportunity again to rediscover their value for worship, for theology, for preaching and for understanding the Christian faith. It is towards this end that this small book is dedicated.

Howard Wallace
November 1993

Introduction

WHEN WE READ, SING OR PRAY from the Book of
Psalms, not only do we encounter a body of prayers
and hymns which come from and spoke to the lives
of faithful ancient Israelites and early Jews, but we
find prayers and hymns which have been and are
still used within the Christian faith.

It has frequently been noted that John Calvin
called the Book of Psalms an 'anatomy of the soul
articulating every facet of cost and joy of the life
with God'.[1] Martin Luther also remarked:

> Hence it is that the Psalter is the book of all the
> saints; and everyone, in whatever situation he
> may be, finds in that situation psalms and words
> that fit his case, that suit him as if they were put
> there just for his sake, so that he could not put it
> better himself, or find or wish for anything better.[2]

Those who study the Book of Psalms must therefore keep in mind that we are dealing with ancient prayers and hymns. We must also recognise that the Psalms can and are used by modern people as a source for prayer and meditation. Our study of the psalms must proceed with these two factors kept in mind.

The organisation of the Book of Psalms

The Book of Psalms is really an anthology, or collection, of the hymns and prayers of ancient Israel. It is in turn divided into five 'books', each of which is concluded by a doxology. These books are:

Book I:	*Psalms 1 to 41*	**Doxology:**	*Psalm 41, verse 13*
Book II:	*42 to 72*		*72, verses 18, 19*
Book III:	*73 to 89*		*89, verse 52*
Book IV:	*90 to 106*		*106, verse 48*
Book V:	*107 to 150*		*150*

However, even within this five 'book' structure, it is clear from other evidence that the Book of Psalms is the result of an extremely complex process. There are many groups of psalms within the whole collection. These include Psalms 1 to 41, called the 'Yahwistic psalms' because of the dominant use in those psalms of the name *Yahweh* (translated 'Lord' in English Bibles). In Psalms 42 to 83, frequently called the 'Elohistic' psalms, the word *Elohim* is used most often to refer to God.

Other sub-collections of psalms can be identified.

A large number of psalms are designated in various ways as 'Psalms of David'. These include Psalms 3 to 41, 51 to 72, and 138 to 145 — plus some isolated ones.[3]

Other sub-collections are designated by association with different groups of people. There are the Psalms of the Korahites[4] and the Psalms of the Asaphites.[5] These groups were priestly singers or musical guilds (see 1 Chronicles 16, verses 4 to 7 and 2 Chronicles 20, verse 19). The sub-collections bearing their names might have originated at sanctuaries other than Jerusalem. The Korahites were at Dan before coming to Jerusalem. Further sub-collections could be noted, many of which are designated by various Hebrew titles.[6]

The final form of the Book of Psalms seems to have been widely accepted from about the mid-first century AD. However, the Book of Psalms by no means exhausts all the hymns and prayers we have in the Bible. Many are embedded in the midst of other works — for example, the 'Song of Hannah' in 1 Samuel 2, verses 1 to 10 and Jonah's song in Jonah 2. Nor did the Book of Psalms comprise all the psalms that were available to Jewish worshippers in the late Old Testament to New Testament periods, as the collections of psalms in some of the Dead Sea Scrolls found at Qumran indicate. The Septuagint, or Greek translation of the Old Testament, even adds a Psalm 151 which is also found at Qumran.

Thus there appear to be many sub-collections, some larger, some smaller, which have gone to make up the final form of the Book of Psalms. The process of collection is still a mystery to us in many of its details. It was evidently long and complex. Nevertheless, while our knowledge of the development of the Book of Psalms is limited, the vitality and continued renewal of the faith that stands behind the final collection is abundantly clear.

Psalm 1 as an introduction to the Book

The suggestion has been made that Psalm 1 (and some would add Psalm 2) functions as an introduction to the whole Book of Psalms. Part of the reason for this suggestion is that this psalm has certain unique features. It does not have a heading or title, and a noted variant reading to Acts 13, verse 33 (in which Psalm 2, verse 7 is cited) refers to Psalm 2 as 'the first psalm'.

If Psalm 1 is intended to be an introduction, then it can be read as a guide to the righteous person indicating how the psalms ought to be read and prayed.

Psalm 1 contrasts the righteous person and the wicked with the Lord's blessing coming to the former. The psalm shows how the righteous one lives. In the psalm, the law or *torah* is shown to be the foundation of personal piety and ethics. The person who is to pray the psalms following needs to be the kind of righteous person described in Psalm 1. Likewise, the life of the righteous person will be filled with the kind of prayers to be found in the Book.

The Psalms and King David

Popular Christian tradition has long connected the Psalms in some special way to David. While the tradition began in pre-Christian times, it has developed over the centuries. Many people, both outside and inside the church, would assume that David was the writer of the Psalms. However, while scholars would seriously question this idea, it is still worth considering the general tradition associating David with the Psalms, for it may help us gain greater understanding of the way the Psalms have been understood.

There are three ways in which individual psalms have been connected with David. First, the headings attached to thirteen psalms refer to specific events in David's life.[7] Most of these psalms appear to be written for an individual who seeks — or, in the case of Psalm 18, gives thanks for — the deliverance of the Lord. The headings are usually associated with periods of trouble or adversity in David's life.

Second, a great number of psalms are connected with David by use of the Hebrew phrase *ledawid* as a title. It is difficult to know how to translate this phrase. The traditional translation, which we find in most English Bibles, is 'of David', taken to mean

'a psalm composed or written by David'. However,
the phrase could be translated a number of other
ways. It could mean a psalm '[dedicated] to David',
a psalm 'concerning David', a psalm 'for [the use
of] David or the Davidic king', or a psalm 'belonging
to the collection of David' — as well as a psalm 'by
David'.[8]

It may be that we have to leave our options open
as Peter Craigie suggests.[9] However, it would seem
at least that the psalms which have headings relating
them to events in David's life presume Davidic
authorship by virtue of the close connection of the
phrase *ledawid* to the description of the event. It is
likely then that for these thirteen psalms, and possibly for others, we still have to keep the possibility
open that the ancient Israelites understood the title
to indicate authorship. This does not mean that *we*
need assume that David actually composed all
psalms with his name in their title.[10] What it does
mean is that some ancient Israelite collectors have
taken the title *ledawid* as an indication of authorship.

Third, there is a small group of psalms containing
direct references to David within the body of the
psalm.[11] These references are mostly incidental except in the cases of Psalms 89 and 132. In these two
psalms, David is portrayed in his role as ideal king
and head of a chosen dynasty.

To summarise, we can say that the attribution of
the psalms to David within the Book of Psalms is

largely confined to the headings and titles of the psalms. Moreover, within these headings and titles there is an ambiguity as to the relation of David to the psalms. It is not certain that David was understood initially as the author of the psalms by those who attached the headings and titles. Note that Psalm 132, which by content is the one which could most easily be associated with David, is not given a title including David's name.

However, while the earliest titles do not unambiguously attribute the authorship of the psalms to David, it is clear that in the development of the headings, certain psalms were interpreted in the context of David's life in such a way as to indicate Davidic authorship of the psalm.

The connection of the psalms to David developed over time. The Masoretic text, or the traditional Hebrew text of the Old Testament, attributes a total of seventy-three psalms to David. This text is the main one followed in English translations. However, the Greek Old Testament (the Septuagint) attributes eight-four psalms to David.

In some of the Dead Sea Scrolls from Qumran, biblical psalms not connected with David in the Masoretic Text or the Septuagint, as well as other non-biblical psalms, are attributed to David. One of the psalms manuscripts from Qumran (11QPsᵃ) credits David with the composition of 4050 psalms.

In the New Testament, this tendency to connect

the psalms with David continues. In Acts 4, verses
25 to 26 and in Hebrews 4, verse 7, Psalms 2 and
95 are attributed to David, even though they are not
designated as Davidic in the Old Testament. Within
early Jewish tradition, the attribution of psalms to
David was also widespread.[12]

Thus there would seem to have been a growing
tradition in which David was not only connected
with the psalms, but was seen increasingly as the
author of them all. However, the question remains
as to whether this growing attribution was simply
an historical claim or whether more was involved
in the process. Some scholars would propose that
the latter is the case.

A.M. Cooper has stated, 'The Davidic attribution
of Psalms. . . is best understood as a productive
interpretive strategy rather than as an historical
claim.'[13] That is, the attribution does not simply
indicate a belief in David as the author of the Psalms,
but rather the mention of David stamps the psalms
with authority and provides a context in which the
psalms can be interpreted by later generations. It
gives a life context — namely, that of David — in
which the psalms can be seen to function as prayers
or hymns in all their different ways for a faithful
person like David.

The attribution of psalms to David can act in an
interpretative role in a number of ways. In the
thirteen psalms where a heading recalls an event in

David's life, there is no special mention of David as a royal figure in the headings and his connection to the psalms does not depend on his royal status. The attachment of the headings to these psalms has the effect of portraying David not in his royal guise, but in the guise of an ordinary Israelite.

Again, in the psalms bearing the title *ledawid*, which come from many different types of psalms, the connection of the psalms with David is taken in a way which sees him as one who uses these psalms as author, collector or singer. The picture of David portrayed is not that of a royal figure in general, but of a man who shares our common human experiences and who has strengths and weaknesses just like any other person.

Brevard Childs has made this point. He writes:

> David is pictured simply as a man, indeed chosen by God for the sake of Israel, but who displays all the strengths and weaknesses of all human beings. . . The psalms are transmitted as the sacred psalms of David, but they testify to all the common troubles and joys of ordinary human life in which all persons participate.[14]

These psalms are thus accessible to the faithful. 'Through the mouth of David, the man,' Childs argues, 'they become a personal word from God in each individual situation.'[15] Thus David as 'author' of the psalms becomes the model and guide for the person who takes up the psalms later as his or her own prayers. The psalms are not just a collection of prayers or hymns offered for the use of the worshipper, but they have been already 'prayed' by David. They are the model for prayer and song in lament or thanksgiving. Hence the use of psalms in the life of faith, and indeed the life of faith itself, are strengthened.

The Psalms and the New Testament

The important place of the Psalms in the Christian faith has its origins in their frequent use in the New Testament. Almost one-third of the quotations from or allusions to Old Testament passages in the New Testament come from the Book of Psalms.[16]

From the New Testament, we can see that psalms were used in a number of ways in the early church. First, they were clearly part of the worship of the early church as can be seen in 1 Corinthians 14, verse 26 and Colossians 3, verses 16 and 17.

Second, the psalms played an important role in preaching and teaching. Over half the citations or allusions to the psalms in the New Testament fit into this category. Paul made frequent use of psalms to argue his point in his letters. Romans 3 provides a clear example where he uses material from various psalms on seven occasions.[17]

By contrast, Jesus is reported to use the psalms in his own teaching in only a few places — for example, Luke 23, verse 46 (Psalm 31, verse 5). However, in many places Jesus is portrayed as using the various psalms to speak about himself — for example, Matthew 21, verse 42 (Psalm 118, verses 22 and 23).

Third, the New Testament writers use psalms to interpret the life and work of Jesus. This is summed up by the statement in Luke 24, verse 44: 'These are my words that I spoke to you while I was still with you — that everything written about me in the Law of Moses, the prophets and the psalms must be fulfilled.' Psalms in this group include those traditionally understood in sections of first-century AD Judaism as messianic (for example, Psalms 2, 110 and 118) as well as others not generally seen as messianic, especially Psalm 22.[18]

Thus, in the New Testament, psalms are used on a wide scale. They played an important part in the development of the worship life of the early church, no doubt a trend carried over from contemporary Judaism, albeit with modifications. They were also important theologically as the church sought to understand the life and work of Jesus.

The Psalms, along with other passages of scripture, helped shed light on the events of Jesus' life. As well, Jesus' life helped interpret anew for the early church the meaning of scripture, including the Book of Psalms.[19]

Twentieth-century interpretation of Psalms

In the twentieth century, major changes have taken place in Psalms study. The discovery of the Dead Sea Scrolls, with collections of psalms on some scrolls, put an end to the idea held by many scholars in the late nineteenth century that the psalms were written in the very late Old Testament period. Many scholars now would see most of the psalms originating in the pre-exilic period of Israel's history — that is, between approximately 950 BC and 600 BC. In addition, there has been great interest in ways to categorise the psalms in order to understand something of how they were produced and in what circumstances.

One of the foremost Psalms scholars this century has been the German scholar Hermann Gunkel (1862–1932). He published a commentary on the Psalms in 1926.[20] Gunkel argued that the original settings of the psalms were not to be found in particular historical situations in ancient Israel, but rather in the worship life of the community. Through study of the traditional language and ideas of poets, their patterns of thought and expressions created for particular situations in society, he tried to establish a correlation between the types of psalms and the various worship contexts.

Gunkel established a number of types of psalms. These included: *hymns*, including psalms celebrating the enthronement of the Lord as king; *laments*, both individual and communal (for example, Psalm 44);

royal psalms, which were connected with outstanding events in the life of the king (for example, the king's enthronement: Psalms 2, 21, 72, 110 and 101; a royal wedding: Psalm 45; or thanksgiving on return from battle: Psalm 18); *individual songs of thanksgiving* (for example, Psalm 69) — and a number of other types.

There have been valid criticisms made of Gunkel's work, but there are aspects which will endure, most notably his attempt to classify the psalms on a three-fold structure of situation, form and content. His contribution to Psalms study this century will remain significant.

A second major figure in Psalms study this century has been the Norwegian scholar Sigmund Mowinckel (1884–1965). He was a student of Gunkel. Mowinckel argued that almost all the psalms were for the use of the community. Gunkel had seen over half as individual psalms. Mowinckel began with a study of the worship practices and institutions in ancient Israel and worked from the types of liturgy to the types of psalms appropriate to them.

His starting point, when focussing on the Book of Psalms, was the category of enthronement psalms. Mowinckel connected these psalms with a specific worship festival — namely, the festival celebrating God's kingship over creation in his enthronement on the day of the Lord at the New Year festival in autumn. Mowinckel drew a parallel for this festival from a Babylonian festival called the *akitu* festival. He considered there to be sufficient indirect evidence to suggest the existence of an enthronement festival in Israel in pre-exilic times.

Not all of Mowinckel's ideas have been accepted. There are some strong arguments against the reconstruction of an Israelite New Year enthronement festival, especially as there is no direct evidence in the Hebrew Bible that such an enthronement festival existed in Israel. Nevertheless, Mowinckel's arguments have had significant influence in Psalms studies, especially in the connection of the Psalms with worship in Israel, the argument for a dating before the Jewish exile, and in tracing characteristic elements in the Psalms to pre-Davidic Jerusalem.

A third significant figure in twentieth-century Psalms study has been Claus Westermann. Westermann is best known for his two works, *The Praise of God in the Psalms* (1965) and the popular introduction, *The Psalms: Structure, Content and Message* (1980). In these he argues a case for concentrating on two major types of psalms: *praise* and *lament*. These are the two 'poles' of human address to God. They are the dominant categories in psalms, all others being included in them. In both categories of praise and lament, Westermann saw that there are community and individual psalms.

Westermann does not identify any one particular worship pattern (for example, a festival) associated with the Psalms, but still sees them arising out of worship in response to specific situations. Praise, for example, arises out of a specific response to the Lord's blessing or activity. Westermann's main contribution, however, lies with his development of the category of psalms of praise and with his theological reflection on praise and lament.

In more recent Psalms study, interest has shifted in a number of ways. While in the past individual psalms have been the focus of attention, some scholars are beginning to pay attention to the Book of Psalms itself, to examine the way it has been shaped and to work out how the various groups of psalms relate together within it.[21]

Another area of interest has been concerned with the way psalms have been interpreted throughout history. The Psalms within their history have taken on a life of their own that is quite unconnected to their original setting and purpose. Patrick Miller has remarked, in relation to lament psalms in particular, that:

> The search for a readily identifiable situation as the context for understanding the laments may, however, be illusory or unnecessary. The language of the Psalms with its stereotypical generalising and figurative style is so open-ended that later readers, on the one hand, are stopped from peering behind them to one or more clearly definable sets of circumstances or settings in life,

and, on the other hand, are intentionally set free to adapt them to various circumstances or settings.[22]

He goes on to note that the 'psalms are by their history not time-bound'. That is, they are not fixed to one historical situation and hence are open to use in many different historical situations. They are also 'by their content not time-bound'. Only a few psalms have references to specific people or places.[23] On both accounts, this means that the psalms are open to use by many people in many different situations.

This is potentially a stimulating area of Psalms study: it allows us to investigate how Psalms interact with people's lives and what the limits are in their functioning in liturgy, devotion, worship, hymns, prayers, sermons and theology.

An important and prolific contributor to current Psalms study has been Walter Brueggemann. In his small and helpful commentary on selected psalms, Brueggemann sees Psalms speaking to people in situations of orientation (hymns), disorientation (laments) and reorientation (thanksgiving psalms etc.). He argues the Psalms incorporate both sides of the life of faith: praise on the one hand, and anger or doubt on the other. They are addressed to God, yet at the same time they are 'God's good word addressed to God's faithful people'.

Brueggemann seeks to evaluate the psalms in

such a way that the devotional and critical traditions support and correct each other. So the critical study of the Psalms with its interest in structure, content, purpose and situation is coupled with the recognition of the psalms as expressions of faith and as resources for faith. Individual psalms are to be understood in the context of the whole Book of Psalms.[24]

So, Brueggemann says, just as life consists of a cycle of seasons of well-being, hurt, alienation, suffering, surprising joy or redemption, we find the psalms encompassing all this experience. Our approach to the psalms, therefore, must be in the context of the whole canon of the psalms which covers the whole range of people's experience of faith.[25]

The language of psalms

In any study of the psalms, the language in which they are written must be attended to carefully. Peter Craigie, in his commentary on Psalms 1 to 50, remarks:

> Thus the psalms, which in many different ways reflect the relationship between Israel and God, utilise the medium of poetry to convey insight, experience, the perception of God and the nature of the relationship with God. They are, on the one hand, profoundly theological writings: on the other hand, they defy any attempt to reduce them to theological dogma or creed. Poetry, like

music, may be analysed and dissected, yet ultimately it must be appreciated and experienced, and to divorce the element of subjectivity from the understanding of poetry is to divest it of its power.[26]

Thus the psalms are to be analysed and to be read as poetry. Poetry is an art form. Unlike prose where there is a logical ordered sequence to the train of thought, poetry operates much more on the aesthetic level. While there is a certain logic in the argumentation within many poems, the techniques for developing that logic must be appreciated. Moreover, an appreciation of the aesthetics of the poem needs to be at every level of the poem, from line to stanza to the whole poem.

Poetry employs language more full of metaphor, symbol and imagery than prose. It does not try to express everything about its subject, but to give the idea of completeness within brevity. Of course, some prose can exhibit features we associate with poetry. In Hebrew literature, it is sometimes difficult to distinguish sharply between high prose and poetry.

While Hebrew poetry has some features in common with English poetry, there are many ways in which it differs. The main element of Hebrew poetry, also evident in other Ancient Near Eastern poetry, is what has become known to scholars as *parallelism*. Parallelism is a way of expressing a single idea in a variety of ways which are closely tied together. A parallel line consists of two (or more) parts which relate to each other. The second part serves to make the thought of the first part more specific or particular, or to expand on it in some way.

Some examples of parallel lines include the following. Note that the Hebrew has been translated word for word so that, while the translation is not good English expression, it does convey the parallelism in the Hebrew. You might compare the translations of the same verses in your own Bible.

Example 1: Psalm 24, verses 1 and 2
To the Lord is the earth and its fullness;
the world and its inhabitants.
For he upon the seas has founded it;
upon the rivers has established it.

Example 2: Psalm 1, verse 6
For the Lord knows the way of the righteous,
but the way of the wicked perishes.

Example 3: Psalm 29, verses 1 and 2
Ascribe to the Lord, O gods,
ascribe to the Lord glory and strength;
ascribe to the Lord the glory due his name;
worship the Lord in holy array.

The parallelism operates in a different way in

each example. In the example from Psalm 24, the halves of each pair of lines say essentially the same thing. However, in the example from Psalm 1, the half-lines say opposite things. Nevertheless, the one point is made relating to whom the Lord favours.

The third example, from Psalm 29, is more complex. Each of the first three lines begins with the same statement. The first line specifies who is addressed, while the second and third lines develop the nature of that which is to be ascribed to the Lord. The final line breaks the sequence, thus drawing attention to itself, but at the same time summing up the point made in the first three lines.

Various other poetic elements appear in the psalms. A number of sound effects are used. There are repeated sounds, predominant sounds, alliteration and assonance. For example, in Psalm 1, verse 1, we find an example of alliteration with the first three words employing the same letters, *'ashre ha'ish 'asher*: 'blessed is the person who. . .' These devices can be used in conjunction with other devices. A variety of special structural features can be used in shaping the whole psalm.

We also find many other poetic elements such as repetition of words or phrases, metaphor, imagery, symbolism and onomatopoeia.

Any attempt to explore what various psalms can mean, or how psalms have been used by faithful people, will need to take seriously the words and poetic devices which have been used to create the psalm. The psalms touch us both in mind and spirit. They express our feelings as well as our thoughts. To appreciate them, we must not only seek to understand what they say but how they say it.

Discussion questions

Talking it through

1 Read Psalms 3 and 51. Both are associated
with events in David's life by means of the
headings attached. The biblical accounts of
the episodes referred to can be found in 2
Samuel 15 to 18 and 2 Samuel 12 respectively.

　　Is there anything in either psalm, other
than the heading, which suggests that the
psalms are related to David? Does the
heading actually fit the contents of the
psalm? In what ways?

2 How influential have the psalms been in
your life, or the life of your family or
community?

3 Read Psalm 22 and then Matthew 27, verses
24 to 54 and Mark 15, verses 16 to 39.

　　Do you think that the similarity between
the events surrounding the death of Jesus
and some of the verses of the psalm is

coincidental, the fulfilment of prophecy, or the writer using the psalm to tell the story of the death? See footnote 18 for exact correspondences if you need them.

4 Read Psalm 23. How many different situations can you imagine in which this well-known psalm would be of use to people? In what situations in your life has it been of help?

5 Read Psalm 114. What poetic elements can you detect in the English translation of this psalm? (You may prefer to read another 'favourite' psalm.)

Widening our horizons

1 In what ways are psalms presently used in the worship services you attend? Do these ways help your appreciation of the psalms or not? Are there ways you would like to see them used?

2 Are the psalms only for those who are committed churchgoers, or are these prayers useful for all people? Find examples from the psalms to illustrate what you mean.

3 Does it worry you that King David may not have written all the psalms, or that many were written for formal worship services in the life of Israel? What insight, if any, do you think we gain by knowing about a psalm's situation, form and content?

4 *Praise* and *lament*: How do these two types of psalms described by Claus Westermann (page 24) also reflect something of the way we experience God? Which for you is the dominant reality?

Cultivating the practice of prayer

Give ear, O my people, to my teaching;
*   incline your ears to the words of my mouth.*
I will open my mouth in a parable;
*   I will utter dark sayings from of old,*
things that we have heard and known,
*   that our ancestors have told us.*
We will not hide them from their children;
*   we will tell to the coming generation*
the glorious deeds of the Lord and his might,
*   and the wonders that he has done.*

Psalm 78, verses 1 to 4

Contemplate the mystery of God's revelation
in scripture. Give thanks for the lives of the
many faithful people who have been
involved in the formation, writing, editing,
collecting and transmission of the books that
make up our Bible.
Give thanks to God for his faithfulness in
meeting us in the pages of scripture.
Seek God's guidance as you set out on this
study of Psalms.
Anticipate new understandings about God,

new discoveries about yourself, new
insights into God's relation to his creation
and people.

He chose his servant David,
    and took him from the sheepfolds;
from tending the nursing ewes he
    brought him to be the shepherd of his people
    Jacob, of Israel his inheritance.
With upright heart he tended them,
    and guided them with skilful hand.
                                    Psalm 78, verses 70 to 72

1
Psalms of creation

❦

WHEN WE THINK OF THE CREATION of the cosmos, our thinking is influenced strongly by scientific developments and discussion over the last few centuries. Our thoughts swing naturally to questions of absolute beginnings, of vacuums and matter being brought into existence. We might think of creation out of nothing. However, it is extremely doubtful that the notion of creation from nothing would have been something the people of the ancient world of Israel would have contemplated.

Several texts from the Ancient Near East which have been deciphered over the last century describe the creation of the cosmos not in terms of something coming into being where there was nothing before, but rather in terms of order and regulation being brought to something that was chaotic and disordered. Creation is an act of bringing order to chaos, of bringing into being something which is good where only that which is evil and foreboding had existed. It is often pictured as a battle between the creator god and a sea monster.

Creation in the Old Testament is expressed in one of two ways. The Lord is seen to create either by means of word or by victory in battle over some such monster as Rahab or Leviathan. This latter mode of creation is a reflection of the old mythic accounts of creation found in the Ancient Near Eastern texts mentioned above. An example can be found in Isaiah 51, verses 10 and 11. There the 'victory in battle' myth is accommodated to the story of the exodus out of Egypt. On the other hand, creation by word, mentioned briefly outside Israel, becomes the chief mode of conceiving of creation in Israel in late Old Testament times. Genesis 1 is, of course, the prime example of creation by word.

In the Ancient Near East, creation did not stop at the ordering of the physical cosmos. It also involved the establishment of such abstract things as righteousness and justice. The right ordering of society and even of family and individual life were part of the process. Creation faith in Israel, in particular, was thus a celebration of the Lord's faithfulness and goodness expressed in 'generosity, continuity and regularity'.[1] The created order — the world and its ordered life — was seen as a place in which the Lord's *hesed*, his 'steadfast love', was to be seen and experienced. It was also a place wherein people were meant to live out their lives in consistency with divine love and in response to it.

Creation faiths in the Ancient Near East did not just celebrate the activity of ordering or creating by a god. They also celebrated the nature of that god. In the Babylonian creation story, *Enuma Elish*,[2] the story ends with the creator god, Marduk, proclaimed king and a temple being built for him. Thus creation was also a witness to divine sovereignty and majesty.

The same is the case in Israel. The Lord is not only celebrated as creator, but as sovereign of all creation. This we shall see in the following psalm.

PSALM 33: A psalm for the creator

Psalm 33 is a descriptive hymn of praise.[3] It praises the Lord as both creator of the natural world and as the one who oversees human history.

It is impossible to fix a precise date of composition for the psalm. Some suggest it was written late in Old Testament times because of the apparent reliance in verses 6 to 9 on Genesis 1, along with other reasons. However, this is by no means certain. Neither can we be certain in identifying the specific type of worship service within which the psalm might have been used.

❏ *Invitation to sing a new song*
   (Psalm 33, verses 1 to 5)

The psalm calls the people to praise the Lord (verses 1 to 3). The righteous are to rejoice, to sing and make music on a variety of stringed instruments. The praise of the Lord is not confined to the human voice, but is also expressed in music (compare Psalm 150). The righteous are to sing 'a new song'. Just what this means is not clear at the beginning of the psalm. We will have to wait to see in what ways this psalm is a new song.

Standing over this call is the second statement in verse 1: 'Praise befits the upright.' Worship, as expressed in this hymn, is the proper activity for the Lord's people. Only as the psalm proceeds do we see why.

The reason for praise (verses 4 and 5) follows the call. The Lord is praised because of his upright word and his faithful work. He loves righteousness and justice and his steadfast love fills the earth. Already, we meet various word plays which will fit into the general theme of the psalm. The people called to praise are described in terms also used to describe the Lord's word ('upright': verse 4) and what he loves ('righteousness': verse 5). The one reflects the other. The praise called for is itself the human reflection or response to the Lord's word and work. A mutual relation between heaven and earth is presumed and encouraged.

❏ *Proclamation of the power of the Lord's word*
(Psalm 33, verses 6 to 12)

The Lord's word (verse 4) becomes the focal point
of the next section. By that word, the heavens were
made and their host formed (verse 6). The idea of
the Lord creating by word is of major interest here,
but in verse 7 — with its reference to the subduing
of the waters of the sea in a bottle and the deeps in
storehouses[4]— the old myth of the defeat of the sea,
representative of chaos, is recalled.

Not only are heaven and its host created, but so,
too, is the earth. Earthly inhabitants are called to
fear the Lord (verse 8). As the parallel term 'stand
in awe' indicates, the word 'fear' means worship
rather than terror. The call is based on the word of
the Lord which is seen clearly in its creative role.
The Lord says or commands and it comes to pass.

Some commentators see verses 10 to 12 as a
separate section dealing with the counsel or plan of
the Lord.[5] I would keep these verses connected to
the section on the word of the Lord. The counsel
or plans of the nations (verse 10) and the counsel
and thoughts of the Lord (verse 9) involve words.

More important, however, is the structure of the
psalm. In verse 6, the Lord creates the heavens by
word, and verse 7 follows with its allusion to the
stilling of the Lord's cosmic enemies in the guise of
the seas and the deeps. Likewise, verse 9 speaks of
the Lord's creation of the earth and is followed by

discussion of opposition to the Lord in the earthly sphere (verse 10). This opposition is frustrated and nullified by the Lord. Nothing opposes his word either in the heavenly realm (verse 7) or in the earthly (verses 10 and 11). His counsel stands forever just as his word stands firm.

Thus the theme of the reflection of the heavenly world in the earthly, noted in a positive sense in verses 1 to 5, is echoed in the negative in verses 10 and 11. The counsel of the Lord opposes the counsel of the nations. In this 'reverse reflection', only that which is permanent will remain. The implication is that the upright and righteous, who reflect the Lord's true nature, will stand. This is confirmed in verse 12 where the blessing, or happiness, of the nation whose God is the Lord is stated.

❏ *Acknowledgement of the Lord's involvement in human affairs (Psalm 33, verses 13 to 19)*
In these verses, the realms of heaven and earth are seen as firmly separated, with the Lord enthroned in heaven and humans on earth. The royal implications in the word 'enthroned' in verse 14 are not out of place in the context of creation as we have seen above. The Lord is clearly king over creation. He has put at bay his heavenly foes as well as the plans of humans who would counsel against him.

The power of the Lord is indicated by the poetic parallelism in verses 13 to 15. Three statements are made about the Lord's activity. First, he *sees* humankind, a simple result of his having looked (verse 13). No conclusion is drawn about his seeing. However, in verse 14 we are told he *watches*. This describes his activity in a more intense way. Finally, in verse 15, we are told he *observes* all their deeds. Not a thing escapes this prying god. His seeing involves examination.

At the same time, there is a progression in the statements made about the Lord himself. In verse 13, we are told simply that he looks down from heaven, but in verse 14 we are informed that the one who looks is enthroned — that is, he is king. Connected with that is the fact that he is the creator (verse 15) who has fashioned the very hearts, the seat of planning, within these humans he observes. It is no disinterested or powerless God who looks on. He has a vested interest in what he sees.

The result of the Lord's seeing is not outlined until we reach verse 18. Verses 16 and 17 interrupt this sequence. They express the futility of human power or devices to save the king.[6] Compare Psalm 76, verses 4 to 7, Psalm 147, verses 10 and 11, and Isaiah 31, verse 1. Reference to the earthly king is in contrast to the image of the Lord as king in verse 14.

The implication of verses 16 and 17 is that, when the Lord observes humankind, he sees precisely where his people put their trust — is it in their own ability to determine their well-being, or is it in faith in the Lord?

Verse 18 returns to the theme of the eye of the Lord. It gives a positive conclusion to this section of the psalm just as verse 12 provides a positive conclusion to verses 6 and 12. Both verses come immediately after expressions of opposition to the Lord. Verse 18 corrects the assumptions behind the trust in human power expressed in verses 16 and 17. The Lord's eye is on those who fear and hope in him, both to deliver and to preserve. These are things which the king's confidence in his military might cannot achieve.

Allusions to motifs earlier in the psalm underline the point. Reference to those who fear the Lord recalls verse 8, while reference to the Lord fashioning the human heart (verse 15) recalls the thoughts of the Lord's own heart (verse 11). These recurring motifs of heart, fear, plans and kingship provide continuity between humans and the Lord. At the same time, it is questioned whether there is, indeed, continuity of purpose between them. In many ways, the humans created by the Lord reflect their Lord, but do they oppose him by their behaviour?

❏ *Affirmation of the Lord's steadfast love*
  (Psalm 33, verses 20 to 22)
These verses return to the psalmist's feelings about God. Several words in verses 20 to 22 recall the

thoughts of verses 6 to 19. The motif of 'waiting' in verse 20 picks up the sense of verse 18. The motif of 'heart' is recalled again (compare verses 11 and 15). The desire for the steadfast love of the Lord recalls verse 5 and verse 18. The motif of hope, treated in a positive way in verses 18 and 22, stands in contrast to the vain hope for victory in verse 17.

Thus this concluding section expresses the hope that what is affirmed in faith at the beginning will be experienced in the people's lives once again. They await a full realisation of the experience of the Lord's steadfast love.

❏ An awareness of Psalm 33

We have discussed this psalm as a creation psalm. Although the Lord's creating is only mentioned in verses 6 to 9, we must remember what we noted earlier about the nature of creation in the Old Testament. It involves matters of the order of human society and activity, as well as ones of the creation of the material world. It also involves matters of human faith, hope and desire. As Peter Craigie notes, creation is not an abstract doctrine about origins, but 'deals with the world in its relationship to God, to human history and to individual human beings'.[7]

This psalm calls the righteous or the upright to praise the Lord. The use of the word 'upright' to describe the people and the Lord's word already designates them as those in accord with the divine will. They are called to wait for him with their *nephesh*, 'soul' or, as it might also be translated, 'life'. The worship of the righteous is seen as consistent with the Lord's activity and will in creation. Praise is befitting the upright because their life is meant to be in intimate accord with the creating word of their Lord. Praise is the fitting response to this creative activity.

Finally, there is left the question noted at the beginning. In what sense is this psalm a new song?[8] Surely the call to praise and the recitation of the Lord's creation is an 'old' song, one which has been sung many times before.[9] But to ask whether this is a new song in terms of whether it has anything new to say is to miss the point. Creation is an ongoing process. To sing praise in the context of creation is to continue the whole process of responding to the ongoing work of the creator.

What we say or do in our praise may not be new in the sense of being different or novel. It is new, however, in the sense of celebrating something which is happening now and goes on into the future. It is new in the sense of being our present response to the creative acts of the Lord in our own time and place. Peter Craigie says the phrase in the psalm points to the 'ever-new freshness of the praise of God'.[10]

Other creation psalms

(a) *Psalm 8* falls into two sections. In the first, the psalmist contemplates the glory of God set above the heavens. In the second, the subject becomes the dominion of humankind over the created world. Verses 3 and 4 form the pivotal point.

The wonder of God's work in the heavens reveals the insignificance of humans. But these insignificant creatures are given authority over creation and are just a little lower than God (or the gods) (verse 4). Two things are clear.

First, human dominion over creation should be a reflection or continuation of God's dominion over the cosmos. The twofold structure of the psalm indicates this.

Second, human dominion is only properly exercised in the context of the worship of the Lord of all. Verses 1 and 9, which are identical and praise the Lord, envelop the psalm, reminding us of the importance of worship.

(b) *Psalm 74* is a community lament (see chapter 5), but in verses 12 to 17 we have an example of another Israelite tradition about creation — namely the one where Yahweh is remembered as the warrior god who kills the ancient dragon of chaos, called here Leviathan, as the first act of creation.

This passage is a clear pointer that such a tradition existed in ancient Israel. However, there is no full account of this tradition left in the Old Testament. The tradition found in Genesis 1 becomes dominant in late Old Testament times. For another story relating to the tradition of the battle against the monster, see Job 41.

(c) Psalm 104 is the closest of all the creation psalms to Genesis 1. What similarities are there between the two passages?

The psalm states clearly that all life is dependent on God (verses 27 to 30). Further, it stresses that God enjoys creation — see verse 26 where the great sea creatures are made for God's pleasure. This is similar to God recognising creation as good in Genesis 1.

The human response to this should be one of praise and joy (verses 33 to 35). We should note that, in contrast to Genesis 1 and Psalm 8, human beings are not the pinnacle of creation in Psalm 104, but rather just part of the web of life created by God.

Discussion questions

Talking it through

1 In what other ways can we praise God beside ways that involve only words (Psalm 33, verse 2)?

2 Psalm 33, verse 12 says: 'Happy is the nation whose God is the Lord, the people whom he has chosen as his heritage.' Compare Psalm 1, verse 1. Many faithful people are not particularly happy or blessed in their circumstances.

How are we to understand the blessing of the Lord in a world where faithfulness appears not to be an avenue to well-being?

3 What are the modern equivalents to the 'horses' and 'strength of armies' in which humans put their trust, both in military and non-military terms (verses 16 and 17)?

4 Psalm 33, verses 16 to 17 state that trust cannot be placed in human power to deliver.

There are many instances today where human power is victorious and secures 'peace' for those with power.

In what sense can we accept the point of verses 16 to 18? In what ways, if any, can we see the Lord delivering and preserving those whose hope is in the Lord's steadfast love?

5 Some people might interpret the deliverance and preservation of the Lord mentioned in Psalm 33, verse 18 purely in a spiritual sense. Do you agree with this approach?

Widening our horizons

1 Interest in the well-being of the environment has increased greatly in recent decades. Questions of the survival of our world are being asked in scientific laboratories, in political debates and in ordinary conversation.

In what ways do some people use an interest in creation to support their own status in society? What has Psalm 33 to say to our modern discussion on the environment?

2 Modern thoughts of creation are often linked with science, physics and astronomy. In the Old Testament, creation is linked with the course of human affairs. Does this modern focus on scientific aspects of creation distort our view of the world in any way?

3 How would an understanding of the statements about nationhood outlined here help you if you were:
(a) a Foreign Minister?
(b) a UN negotiator in a world troublespot?
(c) a guerilla fighter against an unjust government?

Cultivating our prayer life

For the word of the Lord is upright,
and all his work is done in faithfulness.
He loves righteousness and justice;
the earth is full of the steadfast love
of the Lord.

Psalm 33, verses 4 and 5

Give praise to the Lord for the wonders
of creation in the universe,
in the world of nature,
in human society and relationships,
in your own life.
Pray for the healing of our environment,
the resolution of international conflicts,
the provision of needs for all people, and
for a truly peaceful life in our society.

Our soul waits for the Lord;
he is our help and our shield.
Our heart is glad in him,
because we trust in his holy name.
Let your steadfast love, O Lord, be upon us,
even as we hope in you.

Psalm 33, verses 20 to 22

2
Psalms of *torah*

❦

THE HEBREW WORD *TORAH* is often translated by
the word 'law' in English bibles. This translation
does not carry all the connotations present in the
Hebrew word. The English word 'law' speaks to
us about regulations that govern our behaviour,
about the agencies which ensure the adherence of
people to those regulations, or about those who
punish them when they step out of line. However,
the Hebrew word *torah* is better rendered 'direction'
or 'instruction'. What is included in *torah* is not just
regulation, but teaching about the way of God and
about God's people.

Even when *torah* can be associated with the nar-
rower sense of regulation and rule, we need to
understand within what context it operated. It is
helpful to look at how law codes functioned in the
Ancient Near East before we turn to Israel's *torah*.

Law codes generally

Archaeologists have unearthed many extensive law codes from the Ancient Near East going back to the Sumerian civilisation (twenty-first century BC) and including codes from the Babylonians, the Egyptians and the Hittites.[1]

The most famous ancient law code is that of the Babylonian king Hammurabi (c. 1728-1686 BC). The original copy of his law code can be seen today in the Louvre in Paris. It is inscribed on a large, smoothed, basalt rock. At the top, there is a relief showing king Hammurabi receiving the law code from the sun-god Shamash. This indicates that in the Ancient Near East laws were not considered pieces of agreed human legislation, nor were they necessarily a record of the legal practice of the day. Rather, a law code was considered a statement of the divine order. The law code indicated how the gods wished human beings to conduct their affairs and thus ensured that human activity, whether of king or slave, was in accord with the divine will.

This understanding of law was also connected with the concept of creation. In the Ancient Near East, the gods created the world and hence established an order for it that was just. Law was given by gods to humans through the king to ensure the regulation of life within the world accorded with the divine order and justice. The king, as chief servant of the gods, was responsible for the administration of that divine justice in his land.

This seems also to be the Israelite view of *torah*. Old Testament scholar Richard Clifford has said: 'If the Mesopotamian codes were primarily statements of divine justice and royal duty, the Israelite codes are probably to be interpreted in the same way. They defined divine justice for Israel. They do not necessarily record day-to-day legal custom.'[2]

Not only is the *torah* connected with the *concept* of creation in the Old Testament; it is also connected with the *orderliness* of creation and of God's *sovereignty* in creation. In Hosea, 4, verses 1 to 3, the violation of *torah* leads to a breakup of creation. Walter Brueggemann says: 'The good order of creation is concretely experienced in Israel as the *torah*. The torah is understood not simply as Israelite moral values, but as God's will and purpose, ordained in the very structure of life.'[3] This relation of creation to *torah* helps in our understanding of Psalm 19.

PSALM 19: A psalm of *torah*

C.S. Lewis has said: 'I take this to be the greatest poem in the Psalter and one of the greatest lyrics in the world.'[4] It has found a definite place in Christian worship, or at least parts of it have. Verses 7 to 14 regularly occur in church lectionaries. Verse 14 is often singled out as a prayer for illumination. The whole psalm has been the inspiration for more than one hymn.

Most commentators divide Psalm 19 into two sections: verses 1 to 6 and verses 7 to 14.[5] The subject matter clearly changes after verse 6 from an expression of the glory of God seen in the canopy of space to a psalm which focuses on the 'law of the Lord.' In fact, the division is so sharp that Psalm 19 is often treated as though it were two psalms. However, I would not want to be so quick to split the psalm. I believe that each of the two main sections can be further subdivided into two parts.

Verses 1 to 6 break up into verses 1 to 4a which consist of a hymn based on a reflection on creation, especially the starry sky. Verses 4b to 6 is a song in praise of the sun. Commentators have suggested that these verses could possibly be an ancient hymn to the sun-god adopted for Israelite use. Hymns to the sun-god can readily be found right throughout the Ancient Near East — in Egypt, among the Hittite literature, and in Mesopotamia.[6] If verses 4b to 6 are indeed based on such an old hymn, they have nevertheless been thoroughly adapted to the context of Israelite religion, the sun being seen as controlled by Israel's God (verse 4b).

Finally, verses 7 to 14 can also be subdivided into verses 7 to 10, which focus on the praise of *torah*, and verses 11 to 14, which constitute a personal prayer of supplication.

Thus the division of Psalm 19 into two distinct psalms is too simple. Moreover, when we look at the different subdivisions, we note that there are certain connections between them. There are word connections between the sections (for example, 'hid' and 'hide' in verses 6 and 12, and 'heart' in verses 8 and 14). In addition, the theme of 'speech' ties the psalm together (for example in verses 1, 2 and 14, and presumed in the words 'precepts' and 'commandments').

These connections invite us to consider the psalm as a unity. What is more, when we do consider it in its final complete form, we find it yields meanings not to be found if the two halves are taken separately.

❏ *In creation, the heavens tell the glory of God (Psalm 19, verses 1 to 4a)*
In verse 1 the heavens, or the dome of the sky, declare the glory of God. That glory is to be seen clearly in God's handiwork — that is, God's creation. Day and night are full of this proclamation (verse 2), but the paradoxical thing is that this speech is silent. The 'voice' of creation pervades every nook and cranny of the earth, but it is not a voice that can actually be heard. There are no words and no audible voice. The psalmist observes the beauty and wonder of the sky, and interprets it as reflecting God's glory.

Such reflections in the ancient world are a part of what modern scholars call 'wisdom literature'. Much wisdom literature, for example as found in many sections of the Book of Proverbs, discusses aspects of creation and what can be gained for human edification by observing birds, animals and so on (see Proverbs 6, verses 6 to 9). By observing various aspects of nature, God's wise instruction is revealed. In Psalm 19, God's glory is displayed in the marvels of the skies.

❏ *In creation, a tent is provided for the sun*
   (Psalm 19, verses 4b to 6)

While this section reflects something of a wider Ancient Near Eastern mythic background, as mentioned above, it is thoroughly anchored in a context which addresses Yahweh, the God of Israel (verses 7 to 14). The sun is pictured first as a bridegroom coming forth from his wedding canopy (verse 5a) and then like a strong warrior (verse 5b). Each proceeds on his destined journey.

In the Ancient Near East, the sun-god was perceived as a god of judgment from whom nothing was hid as he pursued his set path. The theme of pervasiveness is clear and ties this section to verses 1 to 4a, where the word of creation that reaches everywhere spreads forth the knowledge of God.

Added to this theme of pervasiveness is the theme of judgment — 'nothing is hid from its heat' (verse 6). This judgment is not that of some other god or entity, but of the God of Israel who sets the tent for the sun in the heavens (verse 4b). The sun is in continuity with the rest of creation. The glory of God and his handiwork are proclaimed, but this is coupled with his judgment of all that goes on in creation.

❏ *By* torah *the Lord speaks*
  (Psalm 19, verses 7 to 10)

The focus of the psalm changes dramatically in verses 7 to 9 with a catalogue of the qualities of the *torah*. Six separate words are used in the Hebrew to describe the subject of this section, the word *torah* plus five others. They are translated by six separate English words: law, decrees, precepts, commandment, fear, ordinances. The distinction we might make between some of these words in English ought not to preoccupy us. The effect is meant to be cumulative.[7] We are meant to gain a total appreciation of God's *torah*, its nature and effect on our lives.

The *torah* is perfect, sure, right, clear, pure, enduring, true and altogether righteous. It revives, makes wise, rejoices the heart and enlightens the eyes. In verses 7 to 8, each effect of the *torah* on humans is matched to a statement about the *torah*. However, in verse 9 our focus is on the *torah* alone.

When verse 10 returns to the subject of human action, it is solely in terms of human desire for this *torah*. It is more desirable than the best gold, sweeter than honey. The *torah* of God brings life to humans. As such, it is to be desired.

But note that the focus in these verses is on the

torah of God at all times. The *torah* is not simply given for the benefit of humans as if they were the focus of attention. It is of immense value in its own right, both for what it does and for what it is.

❏ *By* torah *is God's servant warned*
   (Psalm 19, verses 11 to 13)
Verses 11 to 13 continue on from verses 7 to 9 presuming the subject of *torah* in verse 11. The focus now shifts more directly to the human response to *torah*. Even so, it should be noted that humans are always seen as dependent on *torah*. It warns them. They are ignorant of their own faults and are dependent on God for preservation from sin. The psalmist seeks God's protection. Of course, the implication of verse 11 is that *torah* is the means by which God can provide that protection. Only by observance of it can the servant of God become like *torah* itself, blameless and innocent (verse 13).

Verses 11 to 13 highlight the theme of judgment in human life. This recalls the theme of judgment that lies in the mythological background to the reference to the sun in verses 4b to 6. This helps tie the sections of the psalm together further. But the theme of the pervasiveness of the word of God is also present, cementing the inner connections within the whole psalm. Just as the knowledge of God pervades the world and nothing is hid from its searching rays (verse 6), so the psalmist lets *torah* pervade his or her life in being warned, blessed, reproached and protected. *Torah*, like creation itself, carries forward the revelation of God. But also note that *torah*, like the sun, can become the object of praise. In Psalm 19, however, they both point beyond themselves to their creator.[8]

❏ *By 'the words of my mouth', the psalmist*
   responds to torah *(Psalm 19, verse 14)*
In verse 14, the psalm comes back to the theme of words, this time the words of the psalmist. Although in talking about *torah* the psalm has been speaking about another set of words, verse 14 continues the focus of verses 11 to 13 on the human response to *torah*.

The psalmist prays that my words may match the words of God who is 'my rock and my redeemer'. But this mention of the psalmist's words returns us to the words of creation which declared the work of God (verses 1 to 4a). In effect, the psalmist prays that 'my words' will be in concert with the silent voice of creation as well as with the word God has given to his people.

Conclusion

There is a parallel between verses 1 to 6 and 7 to 13. A knowledge of God is provided by both the order of creation and the ordering principle of life. As the sun is a symbol of the created order of the cosmos, so the *torah* is an expression of the created order of human life. Moreover, just as the heavens speak, albeit silently, about the glory of God, so *torah*, through its words, speaks about the way of God. Revelation in its varied forms is the thought at the heart of both halves of the psalm. God shows himself to us in both creation and *torah*. Michael Fishbane says:

> Revelation is the psalmist's access to God and creation; it is also the way in which he — as an Israelite — is singled out. Man gives praise to God the creator by fulfilling his will as Revealer.[9]

But also, in verses 11 to 14, the psalmist is aware of the need of redemption. The psalmist is not in some pure, automatic relation with God. The sun as well as the *torah* search the psalmist out. There are two sides to the praise of *torah* just as there are two sides to the observance of the beauty of creation. Nevertheless, for the psalmist the praise of God in creation and in *torah* sets the context for hope and generates confidence. Fishbane goes on to say:

> . . .it is the mystery inherent in the process of prayer that an answer is, in fact, given; it is an answer expressed in and through the very capacity of the psalmist to voice his anxiety. The grace of a petition-prayer is the gift of hope received in the very process of recitation.[10]

The process of recitation of the nature of *torah* not only reminds the psalmist that the *torah* is judge, that which reveals faults, but it is also the psalmist's hope in that it offers the possibility of living a life in harmony with the way of God. The psalmist has the opportunity to observe the words of the *torah* and to desire that his or her own words may be acceptable to God.

In such circumstances, the psalmist, then, would live in harmony with creation.

Other psalms of *torah*

(a) Psalm 1, as well as being an introduction to the Book of Psalms, is a *torah* psalm. It contrasts the way of the wicked with the way of the one who meditates on the Lord's *torah* continually. It does this by likening the faithful one to an evergreen tree planted by a stream. It is fed, it prospers and gives fruit in due season. By contrast, the wicked are likened to chaff, blown about by the wind. The faithful like the tree will stand, but the wicked will not.

(b) Psalm 119 is the longest psalm of all, with twenty-two sections each of eight lines. The lines in the first section all begin with the first letter in the Hebrew alphabet and the psalm works its way through, so that the lines in the last section all begin with the last letter in the Hebrew alphabet.

Moreover, almost every line says something about

torah or one of the synonyms for *torah*. The psalm is meant to be, perhaps, a statement of everything that there is to be said (from 'A' to 'Z') about *torah*; or perhaps a kind of mantra, a repeated meditation, focusing sharply the hearer's thoughts. Or perhaps completeness, length and constant structure are meant to be reflective of the nature of *torah* itself.

Saying this long psalm draws the faithful one into an act of commitment and devotion which parallels that person's commitment to *torah* in their whole life.

Discussion questions

Talking it through

1 To what extent as Christians can we say with the psalmist: 'The heavens declare the glory of God'? What *can* we learn about God from observing nature? What things do we understand about God that we *cannot* learn from observing nature? Compare Romans 1, verse 20 and Hebrews 1, verses 1 to 3.

2 If Paul says that as Christians we are no longer under the Law in the Old Testament sense (Romans 7, verse 4), in what ways can verses 7 to 13 be true for us?

3 Christians can often develop a negative view of Old Testament law from reading isolated verses in Paul's letters. Do you think that this psalm can add a more positive dimension to our thinking about the role of law in the Old Testament (compare Deuteronomy 6, verses 1 to 9 and 20 to 25)?

4 Can we relate Jesus Christ as the Word of God (John 1, verse 14) to the words of creation that praise God in the psalm?

5 Is there a risk of a superficial understanding of Psalm 19, verses 11 to 13 being assumed which focuses only on the reward and punishment mentioned for keeping or not keeping the law?

Psalm 73 could also be understood in this sense. Do the words of Psalm 19 guard against such a superficial reading in any way?

Widening our horizons

1 Interest in the environment, animal welfare, the preservation of natural flora and fauna and such like is shared by Christians and non-Christians alike.

What difference can our faith in God make to our attitude to the non-human creation? Do you know of instances where declarations of faith have been used to support an attitude to the environment that has proved to be detrimental?

2 In this century there has been a revolution in how we think about 'the heavens'. Scientists and the public talk about pulsars, black holes, gravity waves and the 'big bang'. The sheer size of the known universe and yet the intricacy of its minutest detail are extraordinary.

What does our twentieth-century view of 'the heavens' declare to us about God?

3 Not all those who keep God's 'laws' are greatly rewarded (verse 11). Think through how you might explain this to someone wrestling with the problem. Is every evil that befalls a person to be explained as the result of sin?

Cultivating the practice of prayer

The heavens are telling the glory of God;
and the firmament proclaims his
handiwork. . .
The law of the Lord is perfect, reviving the soul;
The decrees of the Lord are sure, making wise
the simple.

Psalm 19, verses 1 and 7

Give thanks to God for his word as 'heard' in
creation, in scripture and in the life and work
of Jesus. Pray for all who hear that word,
study it, interpret it and proclaim it.
Pray that God's word may bring life to the
communities with which you live and work
and that it may judge all that is unjust, corrupt,
or which does not lead to an honest peace.

Let the words of my mouth and
the meditation of my heart
be acceptable to you,
O Lord, my rock and my redeemer.

Psalm 19, verse 14

3
Psalms of history

MUCH OF THE LITERATURE of the Old Testament is about the world of human affairs. God is most often seen to be active in the realm of human history. This is in contrast to some other Ancient Near Eastern religions where there is a good deal of interest in 'heavenly' things as opposed to the world of human events.

While the Book of Psalms is primarily concerned with prayer, petition and praise of God, many individual psalms make reference to parts of Israel's history. Psalms 78, 105, 106, 135 and 136 in particular devote lengthy sections to the recitation of events in Israel's history. The events mentioned chiefly belong to the period of the exodus from Egypt and the occupation of the land of Canaan. These early events are referred to by the use of a number of Hebrew words in the Old Testament, variously translated as the 'wonders', 'righteous deeds', 'loyal acts' or 'acts of faithfulness', and 'mighty deeds' of the Lord.

The actual lists of events recalled within these psalms, while mostly pertaining to the same historical period, the exodus, are not always the same. For example, *Psalm 105* begins in the period of the ancestors (verses 12 to 15), concentrates on Joseph (verses 16 to 22), then Egypt and the plagues (verses 23 to 36) and ends its historical recall with the possession of the land of Canaan (verses 43 to 45).

Psalm 136 begins in verses 4 to 9 by discussing creation in terms reminiscent of Genesis 1. It then jumps over the ancestral period to the exodus and the Red Sea (verses 11 to 16), the wilderness period (verses 17 to 20) and finally to the possession of the land (verses 21 to 22).

Psalm 78, on the other hand, recalls the captivity in Egypt, the wilderness, the plagues in a mixed order and finally focusing on the reign of King David (verses 67 to 72).

It is clear that the psalmists who composed these long psalms were not interested primarily in getting the history of Israel 'right' in the sense of establishing a definite order of things. Rather, they selectively told their history, as we all do, in order to make certain points to their audience.

The act of recalling these deeds can have an instructional purpose (Psalm 78, verses 1 to 4). But the recalling of the early events of Israel's history and God's part in them can have other purposes as we see when we read on in Psalm 78 (verses 5 to 8). The psalm is being told so that the next generations will hope in God and not be stubborn and rebellious like their ancestors (verses 7 and 8).

The recalling of Israel's history can become part of an expression of praise, thanksgiving, trust or lament. Whatever the case, it should be noted that, when Israel recalls its history, it is nearly always done in such a way that the *hesed* (faithfulness or steadfast love) of the Lord is highlighted. That past faithfulness, as it is remembered again, becomes part of Israel's present. It gives hope for the future.

PSALM 106: A psalm about the past

Psalm 106 is one of the few psalms where we may have a clue within the Old Testament as to how the psalm was used in ancient Israel. 1 Chronicles 16, verses 34 to 36 quotes Psalm 106, verses 1, 47 and 48 in the context of the liturgical act associated with David bringing the ark into Jerusalem.[1] It may be that Psalm 106, along with the other psalms quoted in 1 Chronicles 16,[2] was used in some regular enthronement festival celebrating the kingship of the Lord. If so, this psalm celebrates that kingship by means of confession.

❏ *The psalmist asks God to remember him*
   (Psalm 106, verses 1 to 5)

These verses form the general introduction to the psalm before it focuses on the early history of Israel. The psalm is introduced with an injunction to praise the Lord and give thanks.[3] Verses 2 to 3 then express in positive terms the inexhaustible reasons for praise and the consequent happiness of those who observe justice and righteousness.

The positive injunctions of these verses are then quickly transformed in verses 4 to 5 with a plea for the Lord to remember the psalmist when the Lord helps the people. The psalmist wishes to see and share the prosperity and gladness of the Lord's people.

Note that the word 'remember' in verse 4a is parallel to the word 'help' in verse 4b. The Lord's remembrance of the psalmist or his people is their salvation. The Lord acts on his memory. Brevard Childs has noted:

> God's memory is not a re-creating of the past,
> but a continuation of the self-same purpose. . .
> God's memory encompasses his entire relation-
> ship with his people. His memory includes both
> the great deeds of the past as well as the con-
> tinual concern for his people in the future.[4]

Thus there is a tight connection within these introductory verses. Praise is central in verses 1a and

2 and the goodness of the Lord is demonstrated in the happiness, prosperity and joy of his people (verses 1b, 3 and 5). Only verse 4 sounds a discordant note with its plea implying that all is not as well with the psalmist and the Lord's people as ought to be the case. More than that, this verse introduces the major motif of 'remembering' which will sound throughout the psalm.

❏ *The people forget God, but God remembers them (Psalm 106, verses 6 to 46)*

The main body of the psalm is introduced by a blunt statement about the people's sin, picking up the discordant element in verse 4. In verse 6, the psalmist declares that both 'we' — that is, the generation of the psalmist and 'our ancestors' have sinned. The psalmist joins the present generation's sin to that of their forebears and prepares the way for the presentation of Israel's history which follows.

Following the general declaration of verse 6, we find a catalogue of specific incidents from Israel's early history detailing exactly how the ancestors have sinned. The first incident is the rebellion of the people at the Red Sea (verses 7 to 12). Even in Egypt, the ancestors did not remember the Lord's graciousness.

The story of the ancestors' failure to understand the Lord's action is told in Exodus 4, verses 1 to 8 and 14, verses 11 and 12. The psalm follows the events in the Pentateuch closely. In spite of the people's rebellion, the Lord is said to have saved them at the Red Sea (compare Exodus 14, verses 21 to 31). He saved them solely on the basis of his own 'name', on the basis of his reputation and nature. The result is that the people praised the Lord. Here is the development of the motif of remembrance (or lack of it) and of the theme of praise — that which the present generation are called to give to the Lord.

Then follows a series of seven incidents or situations in which the people continued to sin against the Lord in the wilderness and after they had entered the promised land. These incidents, and their counterparts in the Pentateuch traditions, are as follows:

1. *Craving in the wilderness* (verses 13 to 15); compare Exodus 16
2. *Korah's rebellion* (verses 16 to 18); compare Numbers 16
3. *Golden calf* (verses 19 to 23); compare Exodus 32
4. *Failure to enter the land* (verses 24 to 27); compare Numbers 13 and 14
5. *Ba'al of Peor* (verses 28 to 31); compare Numbers 25
6. *Waters of Meribah* (verses 32 to 33); compare Exodus 17, verses 1 to 7 and Numbers 20, verses 2 to 13
7. *Apostasy in the land* (verses 34 to 39); anticipated

in various places, such as Exodus 34, verses 11 to 12 and Numbers 33, verses 50 to 56.

It needs to be noted that in this list the psalmist has not followed the order of events exactly as found in the Pentateuch, even though in some detail the psalmist has adhered to its traditions. It is clear that recounting the events in some supposed 'proper' order was not on the psalmist's mind. Rather the psalmist adds a personal emphasis to the telling. The cause of the people's sin is their forgetting the works of the Lord (verses 13 and 21). By 'forget', the psalmist does not just mean that the people had a lapse of memory. To 'forget' the works of the Lord is to be disobedient, to pursue a way other than that of the Lord (compare verse 3). This is contrasted to how the Lord remembers his people and saves them.

As the people continue heedlessly, adding one sin to another throughout their history, the anger of the Lord is increased. At first, we are told that the Lord acted to save his people for his name's sake (verse 8), but increasingly the Lord now acts to punish, if not destroy, his wayward people.

The Lord's graciousness, which (in verses 8 to 11) was so evident in spite of the people forgetting, now seems to disappear altogether. Any graciousness towards the people comes only after the intercession of Moses or Phineas (verses 23 and 30). There appears to be little mercy on the Lord's part in these verses, just as there is no praise of the Lord by the people.

Verses 40 to 46 bring the recall of past events in the psalm up to the time of the writer. The whole catalogue of events and situations comes to a climax in which the anger of the Lord increases to the point where he abhors his people and lets them be conquered and taken into exile. This reference suggests that the psalm was probably written during the exile. It also brings into greater clarity the discordant note sounded at the start of the psalm (verses 4 and 6). We now see that their situation is seen as the result of their own sinful ways.

In spite of the emphasis on the Lord's anger in the catalogue of past sins, verse 43 notes that that anger was tempered by the Lord's compassion and, when his people cried to him, he delivered them. Even in the exile which they were probably experiencing at the time of writing, God has looked upon their distress and for their sake remembered his covenant according to the abundance of his steadfast love (verse 45).

The depth of the Lord's compassion, which tempers his anger at his people's rebellion, is clear. That compassion is not cancelled because of the continual rebellion of his people and their apparent inability to learn from their own history. 'Many times he delivered them' (verse 43). The key to this persistent action of the Lord is his abundance of steadfast love. His anger is not totally annulled, but neither is his memory of his people. The Lord punishes his people for their sin, but his compassion transcends that punishment. The abundance (verse 45) and the eternal nature (verse 1) of the Lord's steadfast love are what constitute hope for the people. It lies neither in their own worthiness nor even in their willingness to confess their sins. Even while in exile, the Lord's compassion is hinted at in the pity their captors have for them (verse 46).

❏ *The people cry for deliverance*
 (Psalm 106, verses 47 and 48)
The people then cried for full deliverance which in this case means return to their home from exile. The promised outcome of that is that the people would give thanks to the Lord and glory in his praise. The repetition of giving thanks and praise echoes the references to these activities called forth at the beginning of the psalm (verses 1 and 2).

❏ *A psalm of remembering and forgetting*
There is a word-play in Psalm 106 focussed on the words 'remember' and 'forget'. A contrast is set up. The Lord remembers the people, or is asked to, in verses 4 and 45. However, in verses 7, 13 and 21 the people forget. The Lord is known to remember his people even when they forget him.

Thus we see that the Lord's compassion towards his people far outstrips their faithfulness. That is the nature of his steadfast love.

Of course, the promise of praise and thanksgiving made by the people in verse 47 could be read rather sceptically. Have not this people promised this before and yet fallen back into old habits? Do the people take advantage of the Lord's compassion for them?

The point of the psalm is not that easy promises of praise will persuade the Lord to be compassionate once again — the Lord knows his people and their ways. The point of the psalm is evident right at the start, although we may not have fully appreciated it at first. The psalm begins with a call to praise. It then proceeds with the people remembering their past sins. History is used as a way of making confession. It is in this context that the people make their further plea for the Lord's deliverance and promise to praise him.

There is nothing cheap about their promise at the end of the psalm. It is made in the context of owning their own past sins and of realising the consequences. They, like their ancestors, have sinned and such a confession of sin, if it is uttered honestly, always functions not just as a confession of past acts, but as a call to act differently in the future.[5]

While the psalm plays on the words 'remember' and 'forget', with the people accused of the latter, we ought not to miss the fact that the very utterance of the psalm with its focus on history is an act of remembering. The initiative for this lies with the community. Leslie C. Allen also makes this point in his commentary when he writes:

> The present generation dare to take these past deliverances as precedents for their own future and to bring their own cries to the God of the covenant. They plead for deliverance and restoration to their land. They vow thanksgiving if their prayer is answered, promising to make Yahweh's praise their pride. The psalm has come round full circle to the theme of praise (cf. verses 1, 5, 12). The community waits upon Yahweh, all too aware of their own sin and its wages, but conscious of their waiting Saviour.[6]

Thus, within the psalm an interesting tension is set up between confession of sin and praise of the Saviour where the two are brought together in the one recital of the Lord's past deeds. Just as the Lord struggles between punishing his people for their sin and still having compassion when he hears their cries, so the people struggle between a desire for the Lord's help along with a genuine promise of praise on the one hand, and their own inability to observe continually the Lord's justice and righteousness (verse 3) on the other. The fact that the Lord's own exercise of justice and righteousness is seen ultimately in the tempering of punishment with compassion reveals more about the nature of his steadfast love.

Such a Lord is worthy of praise.

Other psalms of history

(a) *Psalm 105* has three key words repeated. They are 'servant', 'land' and 'word (of promise)'. They are brought together in verses 42 to 44. If the psalm was written in exile, then it expresses a hope and joy in the Lord who fulfils promises. It is a statement of trust and reliance in the Lord who can act to reverse historical circumstances. As in Psalm 106, that hope and trust bring about a commitment on behalf of the community, but note that in Psalm 105, in contrast to Psalm 106, the review of history is seen in a positive light. Psalm 105 is quoted in 1 Chronicles 16, verses 8 to 22.

(b) *Psalm 135* has a similar overall pattern and list of past acts to that in Psalm 136, although without the refrain. It begins with reference to the Lord as creator (verses 5 to 7), but focuses in the end on comparing the Lord with other gods who, in the psalmist's eyes, are but idols.

(c) *Psalm 136* is known as the 'great Hallel' or the 'great praise' in Jewish tradition. It is recited at Hanukkah and at Passover. The frequent repetition of the refrain indicates that the psalm was probably recited antiphonally — as statement, then response — in ancient Israel. In contrast to Psalm 106, the list of past events has a positive ring to it. That is, history is recalled not for purposes of confession, but as sheer praise and thanksgiving. The greatness of the Lord's steadfast love is seen not only in the saving deeds of the past, but in the Lord's daily care of his people after they had entered the promised land.

Discussion questions

Talking it through

1 Do we always tell history, or even our own histories, from a particular point of view so as to make specific points (compare Psalm 78, verses 7 and 8)? If we tell history from such slanted views, does it necessarily make our telling of the history any the less true? Can you recall any biblical books where the particular slant of the writer is evident in the way the story is told?

2 Read through some of the other history psalms — Psalms 78, 105, 135 or 136 — and note what past events are included. What different emphasis can you detect in each of them? What type of situations do you think the psalmists may have written for, given the emphasis in each psalm?

3 Compare Psalm 106 with Luke 1, verses 67 to 80. What similarities of message do you detect and what differences?

Widening your horizons

1 Do you think your church community recalls the past deeds of God not enough or too much? Are there enough opportunities available in the organisation for this to happen, or are there too many?

   If there are not enough opportunities, how can more be created?

2 What stories are regularly told within your church community? For what purpose are they told? Are they told in such a way that the past is remembered just for itself?

   In what ways could they be retold so that they become pointers for a new future?

3 In worship, we recall in various ways the past deeds of the Lord. What are some of the ways we do this and for what purpose do we recall those events?

4 Jesus' suffering and crucifixion indicate to us that not all suffering is the result of a person's own sin. What other cases can you

think of where people suffer innocently?

What stories from the Bible, from the history of the church, or even from your own church community could be told to address situations of innocent suffering?

Cultivating the practice of prayer

Both we and our ancestors have sinned;
we have committed iniquity,
have done wickedly.

Psalm 106, verse 6

Contemplate the history of our nation and the
history of your own family or community.
Remember its times of sinfulness. Remember
the oppression of particular ethnic groups,
past immigration policies based on racism, our
slowness to respond to the needs of other
nations, the greed of individuals and corpora-
tions, our misuse of the country's resources.
Remember before God how we as individuals
have been affected and shaped, both
consciously and unconsciously, by these events.
Give thanks to God for his graciousness and
his willingness to hear our cry for release
from these past and other present sins.

For their sake he remembered his covenant,
and showed compassion according to the abun-
dance of his steadfast love.

Psalm 106, verse 45

4
Psalms of individual lament

SO FAR WE HAVE LOOKED at two types of psalms: psalms of belief in the Lord as creator and orderer of life, and psalms of belief in the Lord as controller of history and redeemer of his people. We move now to another side of the life of faith as Israel saw it: a large group of psalms often referred to as psalms of lament.

Theologian Walter Brueggemann has made the point that laments are authentic expressions of faith which are honest in describing life as it is often experienced — hard, lonely, hurtful and charged with anger.[1] The people of Israel saw these times, when it felt as if God was absent or uncaring, as faith opportunities. In expressing anguish, despair or anger, Israel always addressed God. It was in God's presence that they expected their hurt to be understood, dealt with, and even used to bring about good.

Brueggemann concludes that the lament is:

> . . .a remarkable combination of honesty and dialogue. Frequently, we are honest but unable to be dialogical or, conversely, we are politely dialogical but unable to be honest. Laments in Israel are both. Precisely the combination resulted in joy and newness, the forerunners of resurrection faith.[2]

Brueggemann suggests that Christians can often be less than honest in facing the hard times in life. The study of laments can be instructive in helping us be more open with God.

The structure of laments

Laments which are spoken by an individual constitute the largest single type of psalm. There are over forty of them in the Book of Psalms. In addition, they are found elsewhere in the Bible.[3] The individual laments are structured around a common pattern of elements.

Bernhard Anderson has outlined them as follows and Psalm 13 is given as an example:

Pattern:	Psalm 13, verse:
Address	1 'O Lord' with complaint
Complaint	1–2 Questions 'how long?'
Confession of trust	5 Past action of the Lord
Petition	3–4 Call for answer
Assurance	*
Vow of praise	6 Implicit vow of praise
Assurance of hearing[4]	*

From Psalm 13, we can see that the pattern is not adhered to rigidly in each psalm, although it is recognisable. We also see that the various elements take different forms and can be shifted in position.

An important and common aspect of individual laments is the change from lament to praise. The transition to praise towards the end is unexpected. Many hypotheses have been put forward to explain it. These include the possibility that the psalmists could have had an inner spiritual experience to help them move from lament to praise. Reciting the psalm itself could be a cathartic experience.[5] The most common explanation is that something is said to the psalmist in the liturgy to effect the change.[6] Some sort of 'salvation oracle' could be uttered by a priest which gives hope and confidence to the psalmist.[7]

Another view says that the shift from lament to praise may not be as dramatic as it first seems.

C.C. Broyles argues that, in the case of Psalm 13, there is an inner logic to the psalm: it does not move to certainty of action, but to a positive vow of praise whenever the Lord decides to act. So the psalmist's view has not changed within the psalm, but a confession of trust is added which sits alongside the psalmist's complaint.[8]

While no clear reason is given for the change in mood, there is a clear assumption in the laments that life can be restored by God and that God is powerful and able to achieve this. The Lord is faithful to his promises (Psalm 12, verse 6). But while we acknowledge this, we are also called to recognise that this hope is not just a band-aid statement covering over the real questions of justice and hopelessness. While we must acknowledge the reality of the hope expressed, it is only finally understood when the reality of the silence of God, the desperation of some circumstances and the reality of death are confronted.

While individual psalms of lament have much in common, it is still possible to make distinctions within them. C.C. Broyles has argued for a distinction between *God*-lament psalms (or psalms of complaint) and *non-God*-lament psalms (or psalms of plea). In the former group, there is a complaint against the Lord that he has not honoured the past praise of his people. In them, there is almost total absence of confessions of trust or any elements whose aim is to praise. In the latter group, the Lord is affirmed as Saviour and asked to rescue the psalmist from some other party which is oppressing her or him.[9]

More radical complaint psalms arise from near-death situations in the individual laments.[10] In the psalms of plea, the psalmist and God are on the same side. In the psalms of complaint, the psalmist must appeal to God who appears to be opposing the psalmist.

One of the intriguing things about the lament psalms is that it is not always clear who is the speaker (often just recognised by the pronoun 'I'), who are the 'enemies' or 'wicked ones', or who are 'the poor'. The precise meaning of these terms is not uniform across the psalms. Moreover, they can be used literally or metaphorically.[11] The identity of the 'I' in many psalms depends on who we understand spoke the psalms and on what occasion. Scholars have suggested it could be the king or any individual in dire straits. The identity of the enemies also depends on who we see as writer. The 'poor' could be individuals in difficulty, people who are the object of charity, or it could be a metaphor for the community.

This anonymity has the benefit of allowing many people to use the words of the psalms of lament to express their own complaints or pleas in times of stress or disaster. Patrick Miller says:

The open language of the psalms invites, allows and calls for interpretation that looks and moves forward into the present and future, as well as for interpretation that looks backward.[12]

What is important and consistent in the psalms of lament, as well as in many others, is the conventionality of the language of psalms. It is this conventionality that allows them to be used well beyond the time when they were written.

PSALM 22: From 'prison' to praise

For Christians, Psalm 22 is the supreme example of the individual lament. It is used in the Gospels to interpret the death of Jesus. The psalm opens in verse 1 with words most familiar to us as one of Jesus' last cries from the cross. It is little wonder then that the psalm, at least up to verse 18, is often included in church lectionaries for Good Friday.

Psalm 22 has a more complicated structure than Psalm 13 or most other individual laments. It consists of three cycles, each of which has a section of complaint, followed by a statement of confidence (or trust in God) or by a song of thanksgiving. As the psalm progresses, the cycles get longer. In the end, the psalm finishes with a prayer of thanksgiving with the psalmist praising God for deliverance.

One writer classifies the psalm as 'an individual lament whose theme is praise'.[13]

❏ *Cycle 1: 'My God, why have you forsaken me?'*
(Psalm 22, verses 1 to 5)

The cry of verses 1 to 2 constitutes one of the most bitter complaints about 'my God' that could be uttered. The psalmist has a double problem. Not only is there need of God's deliverance in some form, but there is the apparent silence of God — a matter which ultimately takes precedence. The juxtaposition of the claim that God is '*my* God' at the same time that God seems so far away highlights the dilemma. The psalmist's cry echoes that basic question raised by many who suffer innocently: 'Why?'

In verses 3 to 5, a change of view takes place. There is a statement of confidence. It focuses on the kingship of God (verse 3). It is followed by a statement concerning the trust placed by the community's forebears in the Lord, a trust which was proved in their deliverance. Thus we see that the psalmist asks the question 'why' in the context of faith. The psalmist knows a larger story than his or her own suffering and that helps put the latter into a broader context.

God has acted and delivered the forebears who cried out to him, so the psalmist sees some motivation to repeat the cry for help and the statement of trust. If the Lord continues to remain silent, he will essentially negate his past behaviour and deny himself as God. Note that in verses 4 to 5, three times the verb 'trusted' is used and once the verb 'cried out [in anguish]'. The implication is that to cry out to God for help is in fact an act of trust and faith.

❏ *Cycle 2:* *'I am a worm, and not human'*
(Psalm 22, verses 6 to 11)

In verses 6 to 11, the basic structure is repeated. Verses 6 to 8 contain a second statement of complaint. The psalmist suffers powerlessness, shame and mocking, but the derision is seen to be all the more hurtful when the psalmist quotes the mockers. It is precisely the psalmist's commitment to the Lord which is derided. The psalmist's condition seems to deny that the Lord shows any concern. The mocking words of the protagonists, 'Let [the Lord] deliver', highlight the inactivity of the Lord. The seeming abandonment by the Lord is reflected in the abandonment by the people. By their words, they put themselves at a distance from the psalmist. God's silence is matched by human derision of the psalmist.

The separation of the psalmist from the Lord is made explicit in the way the Hebrew reads in the psalm. Verse 6 begins in Hebrew as *'But I'*. This contrasts with verse 3, *'But you* are holy', speaking to the Lord. The Lord's holiness, mentioned in the first statement of trust, stands over against the feeling of being less than human experienced by this scorned and despised writer.

In verses 9 to 11, there is another shift back to a statement of trust. Again, the Hebrew words draw a sharp contrast. Verse 9 begins *'But you'*, addressing the Lord. The Lord has been with the psalmist from birth, acting first as a midwife and then (literally in Hebrew) 'causing [the psalmist] to trust' even when still a baby at the mother's breast (verse 9).

This then turns to a plea for the Lord not to be far away when trouble is near, echoing the question of verse 1. He is the only one the psalmist has to help (verse 11). The psalmist thus draws the Lord into the situation and provides motivation for his help. The Lord has been there in the past; why not now? The Lord has been the psalmist's God (verse 10 — compare verse 1), so why does he not act like it now?

An interesting comparison is set up when we look back at these first two cycles together. In verses 4 to 5, the psalmist speaks about *national* trust and refers to the ancestors, the beginning of the nation. In verses 9 to 11, the psalmist speaks of *personal* trust in terms of the beginning of his or her life. So at once a parallel is drawn between the national and the psalmist's personal experience.

❑ *Cycle 3: 'Many bulls encircle me'*
   (Psalm 22, verses 12 to 21a)
The third cycle also begins with a complaint in verses 12 to 18. Now the complaint has become much longer and is filled with vivid imagery describing both the psalmist's oppressors and the situation.

The psalmist's enemies are described as wild animals (strong bulls, roaring lions, wild dogs) surrounding their prey. The psalmist's body feels as though it is falling apart, like water poured out, wax melting, or a dried-up potsherd. In the midst of this comes the statement, 'You lay me in the dust of death' (verse 15). The psalmist also apparently associates the Lord with the experience of suffering. It is a statement of anguish by one whose trust in the Lord has been contradicted by circumstances. Has the Lord joined the enemies?

The cycle is concluded by a further petition in verses 19 to 21. In this case, the petition is slightly shorter than the preceding statements of trust and petition. This puts much more emphasis on the preceding complaint. The petition consists of a number of imperatives in which the psalmist seeks further the Lord's assistance. Several elements connect this petition with other parts of the psalm.

Once again the petition begins in Hebrew with *'But you'*, drawing connections back to verses 4 and 10. Moreover the statement 'Do not be far away!' recalls verses 1 and 11.

❏ *Thanksgiving: 'You have answered me'*
   (Psalm 22, verses 21b to 31)
The second half of verse 21 begins a new section of the psalm in which the psalmist gives thanks for deliverance by the Lord. As we explained above,

why or how this shift in mood comes about is not entirely clear. However, the psalmist does seem to indicate some conscious point of change in verse 21b. The NRSV reads: 'From the horns of the wild oxen you have rescued me.'

The image of the wild oxen recalls the images of the oppressors in the previous complaint. However, the translation of the second part of this sentence is contested. The NRSV translation 'you have rescued me' follows the reading of the LXX, or Greek Old Testament. The Hebrew text reads: '. . .you have answered me'. In this version, the psalmist seems to have had some answer to some personal problems. The psalmist now has an answer where none was forthcoming from God previously.

What follows, then, in verses 22 to 31 is a song of thanksgiving. In this, Psalm 22 is different to most other laments which finish with a brief vow or statement of praise. Here, we have virtually a whole psalm of thanksgiving. In this it is clear that the Lord has heard the psalmist's pleas (verse 24). The psalmist now calls on others to praise the Lord. No longer do evil doers overwhelm, but the psalmist now stands in the midst of a company of friendly faces, the congregation of the faithful (verse 22). All the old allegations about the Lord are countered in verse 24.

In the final verses, the circle of praise moves out from one who was regarded as a worm to the ends of the earth, even to the dead (verse 29) and to the yet to be born (verses 30 and 31).[14] Here again at

the end of the psalm, the themes of the ancestors
and the child return and join in praise just as they
had been recalled in the context of past trust. The
movement in the psalm, whereby trust and petition
are juxtaposed with complaint, breaks out into praise
that reaches to all creation.

❏ *Psalm 22 and the death of Jesus*
The first words of Psalm 22 are those that the Gospel
writers state Jesus spoke from the cross (Matthew
27, verse 46 and Mark 15, verse 34). Frequently
Christians speak of the death of Jesus in relation to
the forgiveness of our sins. Yet if Jesus is said to
utter such words of despair from Psalm 22 on the
cross, does that not show us that the death of Jesus
reveals something else as well? As Jesus is seen to
make that human cry, is he not sharing in the cries
of all who suffer or experience such despair, such
as our psalmist?

According to Patrick Miller, the Gospels point to:

the deeper meaning of the incarnation in God's
identification with all those who suffer and cry
out to God. At least one fundamental meaning
of the death and resurrection is that it is God's
way of dealing with and overcoming human
suffering.[15]

He goes on to say that the use of Psalm 22 in
the Gospels shows that:

Jesus died for human hurt as well as human sin.
The resurrection is God's response to the cry of
the sufferer, the vindication of life over death, the
demonstration of God's presence in suffering and
power over it. It is not an end to suffering. . .
It does tell us that God is at cross-purposes with
suffering, fully present in it and at work to over-
come it.[16]

Other psalms of individual lament

(a) *Psalm 6* bears many of the elements found in
Psalm 13 and others, although again it has its own
arrangement. It even has some terms in common
with Psalm 13. The change in mood is again strik-
ing.

(b) *Psalm 39* is different in a number of ways to
other laments. There are some elements of the
general pattern missing and, unlike Psalm 22, the
psalmist is not so much complaining about the
Lord's lack of interest as about another situation.

(c) *Psalm 69* is another complex complaint with an
interweaving of elements including confession (verse
5). This psalm includes a passage of vengeance
against the enemy which may sound inappropriate
to us. In verse 30, at the change of mood in the
psalm, the psalmist ceases talking *to* God and talks
about God.

Do you think verses 30 to 33 are a quotation or

an address to the congregation? Are there any clues in verses 34 to 36 which might locate this psalm in the history of Israel?

Discussion questions

Talking it through

1 Do you think the psalmist blames God, at
least in part, for personal circumstances
(Psalm 22, verse 15)? Is there a sense in
which whenever someone suffers, God
cannot remain neutral and is involved
in some way?

2 The reversal of the psalmist's perception of
the Lord's reaction to a personal situation is
dramatic. Compare verse 24 with verse 15.
Is such a sharp reversal realistic? If so,
under what circumstances?

3 In Matthew 27, verse 46 and Mark 15,
verse 34 the initial words of Psalm 22 are
those quoted by Jesus on the cross. What
other connections with Psalm 22 can you
detect in the rest of these chapters from the
Gospels?

4 Since Psalm 22 was written long before the Gospels, do you think the connections between the psalm and the Gospels (i.e. the clothes, lots, being pierced and scorned) is simply coincidence, or do the Gospel writers make deliberate allusions to Psalm 22 in order to cast the story of Jesus' death in a particular light?

5 When the Gospel writers state that Jesus quoted the beginning of Psalm 22 on the cross, do you think they mean us to hear that as a single cry of despair? Should it be seen in the context of the whole psalm?

If so, what difference does it make to Jesus' meaning?

Widening our horizons

1 It often seems that our expressions of faith or our prayers to God must be polite, correct, positive, and filled with gratitude. There is no room for expressions of anger, hatred, a sense of betrayal or absurdity. Do you agree?

What do the psalms of lament, especially those of complaint, have to teach us in this area?

2 Christians have always made room for confession of sins in worship services. Do you think there ought to be a place in Christian worship for complaint against God and other people who oppress us or others? If so, under what circumstances?

3 C.S. Lewis has said: 'In some of the psalms, the spirit of hatred which strikes us in the face is like the heat from a furnace mouth.'[17] In some laments, the vengeance expressed by the psalmist against the enemies is very strong.

Read for example Psalm 69, verses 22 to 28 and Psalm 109, verses 6 to 20. Such statements stand in contrast to the Christian teaching of loving enemies and praying for those who hate you (e.g. Matthew 5, verse 44).

How do you respond to the passages of vengeance in the psalms? Can you see any virtue at all in having such passages in the Bible?

Cultivating the practice of prayer

My God, my God, why have you forsaken me?
Why are you so far from helping me,
from the words of my groaning?

Psalm 22, verse 1

Recall the times you have felt alone and
abandoned by God. Speak about them with
God.
Recall others who have or must feel totally
alone in their circumstances. Recall those
who suffer greatly through hunger, poverty,
the actions of others. Speak about these
people before God.
Recall the suffering of all creation through
pollution, exploitation and neglect. Speak
about this before God.
Recall the suffering of Jesus on the cross.
Let God speak to you about his sharing the
suffering of all his people and his world.

You who fear the Lord, praise him!
All you offspring of Jacob, glorify him;
stand in awe of him,

all you offspring of Israel!
For *he did not despise or abhor*
the affliction of the afflicted;
he did not hide his face from me,
but heard when I cried to him.

Psalm 22, verses 23 and 24

5
Psalms of communal lament

THE BOUNDARY BETWEEN INDIVIDUAL LAMENTS and community laments is not always clear. Note, for example, Psalm 129, verse 1: '"Often have they attacked me from my youth," let Israel say.' The whole nation is called to echo words that are expressed as the words of an individual. Sometimes in scripture the community can be represented as a single figure — as has been suggested for the figure of the suffering servant in Isaiah 40 to 55 (see Isaiah 52, verse 13 to 53, verse 12).

Some commentators on Psalms have also suggested that even the individual laments could be spoken by the king on behalf of the community.[1] If this is the case, then all laments in effect would become communal laments. Moreover, the structure of communal laments is not all that different to that of the individual laments. The basic elements of address to the Lord, complaint, petition, a divine response (occasionally) and a vow of praise are present.

But there are important distinctions between individual and communal laments. While individual laments are usually expressed in very general language, in many cases communal laments do clearly indicate events that directly affect the community at large. Community laments usually give little emphasis to the vow of praise, but often contain remembrance of some activity of the Lord with his people from the past. This becomes the basis for hope for action in the present. We will say more about the nature of the event recalled from the past below.

Another difference is that sometimes in individual laments the dread moment of judgment has not yet come. Rather, the psalmist feels threatened in the present situation — for example, in Psalm 7. In the communal laments the moment of judgment has come. It usually consists of some national disaster — for example, Psalm 137 after the exile, Psalms 74 and 79 after the destruction of the Jerusalem Temple, and Psalm 44, which was written either after the exile or after the northern kingdom had been destroyed. The response of lament, therefore, tends to come after disaster rather than being a plea for removal of a potential threat.

There is no clear picture in the Old Testament of a liturgy that might accompany a community lament, but some elements are mentioned in places which fit. These include: a call to lament (for example, Ezekiel 21, verse 12; Joel 2, verse 16; Jonah 3, verse 5); acts of purification (Joel 1, verse 14); the wearing of sackcloth (Isaiah 22, verse 12; Jeremiah 4, verse 8) and dust and ashes (Joshua 7, verse 6; Nehemiah 9, verse 1); weeping (Judges 20, verses 23 to 26; Jeremiah 14, verse 12). Zechariah 7 presents a picture of fasting during the exile. The book of Lamentations is often portrayed as consisting of five laments for five days of fasting during the exile.

PSALM 44: A psalm lamenting defeat

This psalm is the very opposite of the victory hymn. Whereas the latter was used to celebrate victory after battle, this type of psalm laments defeat.[2]

One of the interesting aspects of this particular psalm is that the subject changes several times between the first person singular, 'I', and the first person plural, 'we' (see verses 4, 6, 15 and 16). Scholars have suggested that this might be a stylistic device or indicate a change of speaker.[3] Whatever the reason for the change, it is clear that the verses in the singular are tightly bound into the general thrust of the argument of the psalm. Verse 4 becomes the basis for the statement in verse 5. Verse 6 provides the necessary contrast for the point in verse 7. Finally, verses 15 and 16 depend on the previous verses for context.

It would seem best to take the psalm as a unity regardless of the reason for the change in person. In general, the psalm can be divided into verses 1 to 8, dealing with the past, verses 9 to 22 with the lament, and verses 23 to 26 with a plea for the Lord's help.

❏ *'We have heard with our ears. . .'*
  (Psalm 44, verses 1 to 8)
This particular community lament begins with remembrance of the past. In verses 1 to 3, the psalmist remembers what the present generation have heard about the Lord's deeds in the days of their ancestors. The references in verse 2 are to the Lord giving Israel the land of Canaan and then maintaining them in it. The point stressed is that the ancestors did not trust in their own strength in any of this, but were dependent on the Lord who delighted in them (verse 3).

In verses 4 to 8, the scene switches from the past to the present. The section starts with a direct address to the Lord: *'You are my King. . .'* The psalmist claims the same faith as the ancestors for both him or herself and for the community as a whole. The speaker in verses 4 and 6 is unclear as noted above, but the military image in verse 6 suggests a leader in battle, perhaps the king at the head of his army. In any case, the point made is that the relationship of the psalmist to the Lord is the same as that of the ancestors.

If that is the case then the effect of the relationship should be the same. Indeed, the psalmist claims that they have already experienced the leadership of the Lord in times of battle (verse 5). It has been the Lord's action which has delivered the nation in recent times as well as long ago. The Lord is their boast, the one to whom they give thanks. At the end of these verses, the reader is left with the sense that the psalmist would not be making this claim if something were not drastically wrong.

❏ '. . .you have rejected us. . .'
   (Psalm 44, verses 9 to 22)

Our psalmist does not mincewords in the next section of the psalm. Verses 9 to 16 state clearly what we only suspected might be the problem back in the last section. The psalmist begins with 'Yet you. . .', again addressing God directly as in verse 4. The translation 'yet' does not necessarily carry the force of the Hebrew word at the beginning of verse 9. It could also be translated 'surely', with a sense that the psalmist has a point to make about the Lord's action or lack of it and is not going to let the Lord off the hook too easily.

The psalmist outlines boldly the Lord's neglect of

his people. In contrast to the statement at the beginning of verse 4, 'You are my King. . .', each of verses 9 to 14 begins by addressing the Lord with 'You have. . .', outlining his actions against his people. He has spurned them. He does not go out with their armies. The effect is that the enemies plunder the people. They have become a laughing-stock among the nations. While it is the other nations who defeat Israel, the Lord cannot avoid complicity.

Once again, the military context is clear and we are led to conclude that the national disaster facing Israel is defeat in battle. But these verses suggest more. The references to the Lord scattering his people and selling them for a trifle could indicate the period of Israel's exile after their defeat at the hands of the Babylonians in 587 BC. That context is feasible, although it is also possible that other smaller deportations could have been experienced after earlier defeats. At any rate, the result is a sense of shame felt by the psalmist.

It is important to note that the psalmist feels shame, not guilt. In this psalm, the Lord is clearly seen as the guilty one, not the people. In verses 1 to 8, the psalmist shows that the people have been faithful. It is the Lord who is seen to be at fault.

Verses 17 to 22 conclude this section. The psalmist proclaims the faithfulness of the people in comparison to the Lord's action. The Lord's delight in the ancestors and the faithfulness of the psalmist's

generation have already been extolled. In verses 17
and 18, the innocence of the people is proclaimed.
The proof of it is that the Lord would surely know
their faithlessness if it existed — after all, he is God.
The Lord's complicity in the events confronting the
people is stated clearly again in verse 22.

At the end of this central section of the psalm,
we are not left in doubt as to the nature of the
problem faced by the people. The Lord, by his
inaction, is responsible for the demise of his people.

❏ *'Rouse yourself!'* (Psalm 44, verses 23 to 26)
In verse 23, the plea of the psalmist reaches a climax.
We need to listen to the nature of the language in
these verses and the frustration embedded in it.
Verses 23 and 26 contain four imperatives directing
the Lord to respond. The first three create the image
of a frustrated person unsuccessfully trying to rouse
another from a deep sleep in an emergency situation.
The last imperative makes the clear plea for the Lord
to redeem, to save his people.

There is real aggravation expressed here with the
Lord. The clear message is that the Lord remains
silent when he should speak and act! The silence
of the Lord is as real and as devastating in itself as
is the onslaught by the enemy nation. The Lord is
pressed to answer why he neglects them (verse 24).

The imagery of verse 25 is twofold, recalling the
curses by God in the garden of Eden upon the
serpent (Genesis 3, verse 14) and upon human beings

(verse 19). In Eden, it is God himself who curses. Thus the implication here is that the curses the people bear now can only come from the Lord. Are those who are faithful and innocent to be cursed in this way?

The theme of forgetting emerges several times in the psalm. In verse 17, the psalmist proclaims that the people have not forgotten the Lord and, if they had, would not the Lord know it (verse 20)? Moreover, in the past, both with the ancestors and the present generation, the Lord has 'remembered' his people.

To remember them is to act on their behalf. To forget is thus not just to have something innocently slip the mind, but is actively to abandon another. The Lord's past remembering of his people has been clear in his past action, but all that stands in contrast to the present silence on the Lord's part.

The point about the Lord's forgetting is rather subtly driven home when we think back to the earlier part of the psalm, for there we have a vivid illustration of the *people* remembering the Lord in past action — first, in the sense of simply recalling past action and second, in the sense of acting appropriately.

The psalm ends with the final plea that the Lord act 'for the sake of [his] steadfast love'. Given his nature and responsibility towards his people, he can do no less.

Conclusion

In this psalm, faith is stretched to the boundary. This is so not in terms of understanding, nor because faith is weak, feeble or cannot see the whole of things. Rather, faith is stretched to the boundary here, because it confronts the reality of the silence of God. The psalmist asks the question whether she or he is to be the only voice that breaks the silence. In Psalm 44, the silence with which Israel's defeat at the hands of the enemy is greeted by the Lord puts a question mark next to the Lord's faithfulness, not that of the psalmist.

Some people, when met by the silence of God in the face of personal or communal disaster, see the only possible response as questioning whether there is a God who cares. But that is not the only option. Peter Craigie has remarked, in relation to this psalm, that God is, in fact, the root problem in the psalmist's situation. The answer to the problem is found at the very end of the psalm:

> And so ultimately, Psalm 44, with its concluding prayer, points in the same direction as the Book of Job — namely, that there is an immense mystery in God and his ways, but one must continue to trust and to pray.[4]

There is value in noting the psalmist's conviction in staying with God in this context, but more can be said here. When faith confronts the silence of

God, it can begin to doubt or question itself. On the other hand, it can also brutally confront that silence and the God who is believed to be responsible for it. In such daring, there is the distinct possibility that new understandings of God himself will emerge. We are referring not only to the psalmist's persistence in prayer, but to the courage of confronting God with hard questions.

J. Craghan has applied this to our relationship with God today:

> It is covenant which gives us the right to make such demands. Not to employ such bold language at prayer is to deny our status as a covenant community. We must not allow God to sleep any longer. Disorientation is not desirable for its own sake.[5]

Finally, we return to the question of the past event cited in many of the communal laments and its relationship to the immediate situation of the psalm. In Psalm 44, the context appears to be that of military defeat, possibly in connection with the Babylonian exile. The past event recalled is Israel's first military victory — namely, the conquest of the promised land. Within the psalm, the recall of that event is seen in relation to the demand that the Lord act in the present and come to the rescue of the people. A similar situation exists in each of the national laments.

Richard Clifford has suggested that the psalmist

chooses to recall a particularly powerful event from
the past which is appropriate to the present crisis.[6]
In times of national or military disaster, it is usually
the exodus out of Egypt or the conquest of the
promised land that is recalled — for example, in
Psalms 80 and 83. Psalm 74 recalls the creation of
the cosmos as a demonstration of God's power.

Various things are achieved by this recall. For
example, in Psalm 44, verse 26, the point seems to
be the verification of the Lord's faithfulness and
promises. The threat to the Lord's people is a threat
to the Lord himself. The recall of the past is not
essentially a call to faith on the people's part, although that is not absent. The psalmist does not
just call the people to look to the past and be comforted. Rather, the recall of the past is the psalmist's
way of dealing with the problem of the apparent
lack of faithfulness on the Lord's part. It is a way
of urging the Lord to remember his people.

Scholars have highlighted other aspects of this
referencing to the past. It could be thought of as a
way of making former deeds 'present'. In other
words, it could be the verbal equivalent of a statue
— that is, 'this is like that'. Thus, recalling the past
could be a way of trying to make present the power
of the Lord to deliver.

Also, recalling the past could be a way of recognising the unity and continuity of the saving work
of the Lord — a recognition, in effect, that the mean-

ing of the past is bound to the present and the future. In other words, the psalmist could be saying that the Lord's saving deeds of the past are without meaning unless the Lord continues to save his people.

Other psalms of communal lament

(a) Psalm 74 contains a vivid description of the destruction of the Temple, probably in connection with the sacking of Jerusalem by the Babylonians in 587 BC. Verses 12 to 17 recall God's act of creation.

In ancient mythic thinking, stories about the creation of the cosmos often contain reference to the chief god building a temple after the act of creation. This is probably behind the reference to creation here in connection with the Temple's destruction. Can you think of any other reasons why the psalmist might recall God's creation of the cosmos when lamenting the destruction of the Temple?

(b) Psalm 79 does not contain a detailed reference to a past event in contrast to other communal laments, but in what way does it allude to the past? What event constitutes the present context of the psalm?

(c) Psalm 89 can be divided into two halves. The first half (verses 1 to 18) is a song of praise to the Lord, the creator and sovereign of the cosmos. The second half (verses 19 to 37) focuses on the Lord's election of David and his descendants as king. There are certain parallels in the description of the Lord as king and that of the Davidic king. From verses 38 to 51, can you tell what seems to have gone wrong?

Discussion questions

Talking it through

1 From your knowledge of Israel's history, do you think Psalm 44, verses 17 to 18 is an accurate summary of the Israelites' relationship with God? Is the psalmist arguing a logical case?

2 What evidence is there in Psalm 44 that the psalmist is being honest rather than 'saying the right things'? What do you think of this approach?

3 Why does the psalmist make a final plea for the Lord to deliver the people 'for the sake of your steadfast love' (verse 26)? Is the psalmist's aim to manipulate God or does this cry from the heart reflect something more deep-seated?

Widening your horizons

1 Are there times when you believe yourself or your community to have been faithful to God, or as faithful as is humanly possible, but that God has let you down and been unfaithful to you? What is one such occasion? How did you respond?

2 Do you ever feel like complaining to God or do you tend to think first that:
   (a) the situation may be God's response to some unwitting faithlessness on your part, or
   (b) it is being unfaithful to complain to God?

3 How do you think God reacts to our outbursts of anger against him? Why do you think this way?

4 In what community or global situations does God seem to be silent today? Is he? How do you explain his 'silence' or 'reticence' to be involved?

5 Psalm 44 comes from a military context. Do you think it is legitimate to assume today, on the basis that we are Christians, that the Lord is *on our side* in times of war or other major conflict?

Are there any circumstances when we could make such a claim? What might they be?

Cultivating the practice of prayer

In God we have boasted continually,
*   and we will give thanks to your name forever.*

Psalm 44, verse 8

Recall the past deeds of God in your own life,
    in that of your faith community
    and in world events.
Give thanks for those who have faithfully
'boasted in the Lord' in past times and who
have passed on the tradition of God's care
for his people to the present generation.
Remember the times when you have felt
abandoned by God. Pray for those who are
caught in the nightmare of warfare, large or
small. Pray for those who feel despised and
rejected, especially by God.
Let your prayers join theirs in calling for
God to redeem all people who suffer innocently.

Rise up, come to our help.
Redeem us for the sake of your steadfast love.

Psalm 44, verse 26

6
Psalms of confession

❧

WE HAVE DISCUSSED BOTH INDIVIDUAL and communal psalms of lament. These laments vastly outnumber psalms of confession or penitence in the Book of Psalms. In fact, psalms of confession are rather rare. Only seven psalms are usually included in this category. They are Psalms 6, 32, 38, 51, 102, 130, and 143. The association of these psalms has long been recognised in Christian tradition. Martin Luther treated them together in his commentary on the psalms.[1]

The small number of psalms of confession may seem strange to Christians. We are used to confession as a regular part of worship and many of us, particularly those of Protestant affiliation, have often heard the sinfulness of humans preached or proclaimed. The claims of innocence that come from the psalmists as they complain against God's lack of concern for them seem doubly strange. How can humans be concerned *so little* about their sin that confession plays a minor role and *so sure* of their innocence before God that they have the audacity to proclaim it?

While psalms of confession are rare as a category, it does not mean that confession is totally absent from other categories of psalms. An example is Psalm 69, verse 5. While the psalmist generally proclaims innocence before God, of faithfulness (verses 9 to 12), that boast is not made without recognition of having committed sins against God (verse 5). God knows the psalmist's 'folly'.

The psalmist does not proclaim to be anything other than an ordinary human being with faults and sins. The psalmist's innocence is not based on being holier than God, without blemish, but is based on the fact that his or her faithful and unfaithful acts are fully known. The psalmist does not and cannot hide anything from God. Because of the openness of the relationship in which the psalmist is not dissembling with God, the psalmist believes that God should openly, without impediment, act on the psalmist's behalf.

PSALM 51: A psalm confessing personal failure

This is the most well-known psalm of confession

and is widely used in Christian worship. Verses 1 to 12 are used in the liturgy for Ash Wednesday at the beginning of Lent, while verses 10 to 17 are occasionally used for one of the Sundays in Lent. Elsewhere, verse 15 has been used for many centuries as an opening verse in the daily office of religious orders.

The psalm, sometimes called the *Miserere*,[2] breaks naturally into a number of small sections which are linked in a coherent progression. A number of themes and key words tie the various sections together, for example 'wash' (verses 2 and 7), 'cleanse/clean' (verses 2 and 7), 'transgressions' (verses 1 and 3), 'joy' (verses 8 and 12), 'blot out' (verses 1 and 9), 'face/presence' (verses 9 and 11),[3] 'spirit' (verses 10, 12 and 17 — compare verse 11) and 'salvation' (verses 12 and 14).

The use of cultic language also ties the psalm together. For example, the words 'wash', 'cleanse' and 'blot out' all have meaning in the context of worship. This ties in with the references to sacrifice later (verses 16, 17 and 19).

❏ *'Have mercy on me, O God. . .'*
   (Psalm 51, verses 1 and 2)

The psalmist begins with a basic plea: for God to have mercy. The opening lines have been carefully constructed and set the agenda for the rest of the psalm. The initial plea for mercy is paralleled, but also developed in the last line of verse 1: 'blot out my transgressions'.

The mercy the psalmist seeks is forgiveness.
These two pleas surround two other lines in verse
1 which give the grounds for the psalmist's confidence that this forgiveness can be achieved. The
basis of this confidence is the steadfast love, the
abundant mercy of God. It is on God's mercy that
the psalmist depends for forgiveness. One could
also read from this verse that it is the nature of God's
love and mercy to forgive.

If such is the case, we will see that this does not
mean that God's mercy is non-discriminating. Verse
2 concludes the opening section by expanding further on the last line in verse 1. The psalmist uses
the metaphor of washing to convey the notion of
forgiveness.[4]

❏ *'I know my transgressions'*
  (Psalm 51, verses 3 to 5)
The psalmist picks up the words 'transgressions' and
'sin' from the first section and develops the theme
of personal sin in this section. This sin is something
which cannot be escaped. It is always in the psalmist's mind.

In verse 5, the psalmist adds to the sense of the
all pervasiveness of sin by tracing it back to
childhood, even conception. This is not a basis for
a doctrine of original sin. The psalmist's language
is poetic.[5] The point that is being made is that the

psalmist is not only ever conscious of present sin, but past sin. Knowledge of that sin is constant, not fleeting. Moreover, the thought of the psalmist being a sinner from before birth adds a sense of helplessness in this condition. The psalmist has no personal resources to change the condition.

It is on this last ground that the psalmist turns to God. But the psalmist also realises that the one against whom personal sin has been committed is none other than God (verse 4). Against God and God alone has the transgression been committed.[6] God's judgment against the psalmist is therefore justified.

The nature of the psalmist's sin is not specified in the psalm, but whatever it is it clearly affects the relationship with God. As Walter Brueggemann has said, the point made in the psalm is that sin is primarily a theological problem — that is, a problem concerning God and his relation with us.[7] This is so even when the sin is clearly social.

It is interesting to note that the heading given to this psalm associates it with the episode of David forcing himself upon Bathsheba and then conniving to have her as his wife. The sin in that episode is personal *and* social. While the heading is undoubtedly a much later addition to the psalm, it at least shows us that the editors of the psalms were not averse to seeing such social and personal transgressions as still sins against God.

❏ *'Create in me a clean heart, O God. . .'*
  (Psalm 51, verses 6 to 12)

The psalmist turns back to seeking God's mercy and
forgiveness. The section begins with a statement
about God — namely, that he desires truth ('You
desire truth in the inward being').[8] The psalmist
then asks to be taught wisdom ('teach me wisdom
in my secret heart'). Thus verse 6 stands as an
introduction to the section. Each of the following statements elaborates on how this wisdom might be attained.

In each statement, the psalmist requests something of God: to *remove* that which is undesirable
('Purge me with hyssop': verse 7), to *recreate* him
from within ('Create in me a clean heart. . . put a new
and right spirit within me': verse 10), to *remain* present
with him ('Do not cast me away from your presence':
verse 11). This list of requests develops the imperative style of the psalm already established in verse
1 ('Have mercy on me, O God'). The psalmist
desires to hear joy and gladness again (verse 8) but,
if he is going to remain in the presence of God, then
it will depend completely on God's action.

In the midst of this request, the psalmist remains
acutely aware of being judged by God. It is God
who has, to this point, crushed the psalmist (verse
8). But the psalmist seeks (verse 9) that God will
hide his face from his sins and blot out his transgressions. The reference to 'your face' in this verse
is recalled in almost the identical Hebrew expression

(translated 'your presence') in verse 11. The psalmist seeks to have personal sins removed from God's presence, but not to be personally removed.

The removal of sin by God is not a simple matter and the psalmist understands that. The psalmist is aware of being judged and of total dependence on the mercy of God. When the psalmist seeks the 'truth' that God desires, the wisdom that is gained is, as the psalm makes clear, as much knowledge of being sinful as understanding what is right.

The psalmist also longs for a spirit that is steadfast (verse 10), noble or generous (verse 12). This cannot be separated from the request which comes in between in verse 11 — namely, that God not take away his 'holy spirit' from the psalmist ('do not take your holy spirit from me': verse 11). We cannot simply equate this reference to the 'holy spirit' with the Holy Spirit in the New Testament. What the psalmist desires is made clear by the parallel line in verse 11. The psalmist does not want to be cast from God's presence. God's holy spirit thus relates to the sense of God's presence. In the Old Testament, the spirit or breath is that life-giving force that comes with the presence of God.[9]

The series of requests made by the psalmist and which focus on the psalmist desiring the presence of God contrasts with Psalm 15 and Psalm 24, verses 3 to 6. In each of these cases, the psalmist describes the person who may come into the presence of the

Lord. In each case, the conditions are set for the psalmist and it is the responsibility of the worshipper to ensure their worthiness to enter. In Psalm 51, the psalmist can clearly do little personally to be equipped to be in the presence of God.

❏ *'O Lord, open my lips'*
   (Psalm 51, verses 13 to 17)

These verses outline the consequences of God acceding to the requests of the psalmist. The psalmist vows to teach other transgressors God's ways so that they will return to God (verse 13) and will sing aloud of the deliverance experienced (verse 14). Parallel to this is verse 15: if the Lord 'will open my lips', says the psalmist, then 'my mouth will declare [God's] praise'.

Interwoven with these consequences are statements highlighting again the basis of the psalmist's requests of God (verses 16 and 17). God has no delight in sacrifices, says the psalmist. What pleases God is a 'broken and crushed' heart. At first sight, this could sound like a rather cruel demand by God. Does he delight in his people being humiliated before he is gracious to them? But verses 16 and 17 must be read in the context of the rest of the psalm. A broken and crushed heart is surely one that knows its own sins, seeks cleansing and desires to be renewed by God's spirit.

We are not talking here of a human spirit broken

to the point where it has no vitality left, but rather of a spirit which has learnt the wisdom and truth God desires (verse 6). In the words of verses 10 to 12, we are talking of a human spirit enlivened by the presence of God's holy spirit.

The language of verses 16 and 17 reminds us of other Old Testament passages such as Psalm 40, verses 6 to 10, Psalm 69, verses 30 to 31 and especially Micah 6, verses 6 to 8 — what the Lord requires of his people is 'to do justice, and to love kindness, and to walk humbly with. . . God'. This positive statement follows others which seem to question the necessity of sacrifice for God's forgiveness. But we ought to be careful here. Micah is not necessarily arguing against the effectiveness of sacrifice. There are many Old Testament texts which spell out at great length the detail and purpose of sacrifice — Leviticus chapters 1 to 7, for example. Compare also Psalm 54, verse 6 and Psalm 66, verse 15. Micah's point is not to denigrate sacrifice, but to put sacrifice in the context of a repentant heart within the one who seeks God's forgiveness.

In Psalm 51, it would seem, the statement of verse 17 should also be read in that larger context of Israelite religion. The sacrifice acceptable to God is a broken spirit. It is all we have outlined above. It surely is in that context that any sacrifice would need to be made. The sacrifice would be the outward expression and symbol of the inward condition.

❑ *'Do good to Zion. . .'*
(Psalm 51, verses 18 and 19)

The last two verses of the psalm seem to be entirely
out of place. They introduce the subject of Zion and
seek divine aid in rebuilding the walls of the city
('Do good to Zion. . . rebuild the walls of Jerusalem':
verse 18).

We could presume from this reference that these
verses were penned in a time after the destruction
of the walls of Jerusalem by the Babylonians in 587
BC and before the time of Nehemiah's mission to
rebuild the city in approximately 445 BC. In addition, the reference in verse 19 to right sacrifices
sounds like an effort by a later writer to correct an
impression which could be gained from the earlier
part of the psalm — namely that sacrifices, burnt
offerings and the like were no longer required. In
such a case, there would seem to be little connection
between these verses and the rest of the psalm.
Verses 18 and 19 stand only as a rather crass cor-
rection to the rest.

However, there is another possibility. If the above
presumed date of the addition of verses 18 and 19
is correct, then it is possible that we are meant to
read the whole psalm in terms of the circumstances
facing Israel at that time. The psalm is then read
as one for a period when the old familiar ways of
seeking God's forgiveness and presence are no
longer available. That is, if the Temple, the place of

sacrifice and the presence of the Lord, has been destroyed, then the question arises as to how can Israel seek God's mercy?

One possibility is to focus not on the public ritual of sacrifice, but on the internal contrition of the worshipper. When the visible, public symbols of the faith are no longer available, there can be a refocus on the personal and private elements of the faith. In this case, the call for a 'sacrifice' of a broken spirit is not a rejection of the sacrifice of, say, animals, but rather a *substitution* when they are no longer available. The writer of these verses seeks a time when the interim measures of private and personal faith will be supplemented again by the great public symbols of sacrifice ('then you will delight in right sacrifices, in burnt offerings. . . then bulls will be offered on your altar': verse 19).

Regardless of how we understand the relation of these last two verses to the rest of the psalm, one thing is clear. The psalms were for the Israelites part of a living faith. As it was a living faith, they were always critically reassessing their expression of that faith.

Conclusion

Psalm 51 is a classic text in both Christian and Jewish faiths for the expression of contrition and repentance before God. In the process of reading that confession of sin, we also learn much about the nature of sin and repentance as we have tried to outline above. Not least to be learned from the psalm is the following point, as expressed by Claus Westermann:

> . . .the change brought about by forgiveness which we see here is to be understood as a change to a new and joyful life, in a new and right spirit, through a renewed fellowship with God. It is not seen as consisting in a perpetual awareness of sin or an attitude of submissive penitence.[10]

Other psalms of confession

(a) *Psalm 32* falls quite naturally into a number of sections which form a sequence. The psalmist's conclusion, based on experience, that 'those whose transgression is forgiven', is provided in verse 1. The words sound like the beatitudes of Jesus.

What do verses 3 to 7 suggest is the key to that happiness? What is the cost of avoiding issues of guilt? What choice is offered at the end? Verse 9 could be said in a self-righteous manner. How could that be avoided?

(b) *Psalm 38* combines confession with lament, but does not reach the end of the cycle found in many of the individual laments — namely, the point of a vow of praise or thanksgiving. It does not reach the point of praise or promise to teach others which is found in Psalms 32 and 51.

(c) *Psalm 130*, like Psalm 51, combines individual elements with public matters. In such a brief passage, the psalmist expresses the depth of human suffering from committing sin, the utter hopelessness of humans to rescue themselves from their own devices, and the unutterable joy of forgiveness offered by the Lord.

The psalm also highlights the sense of waiting involved in receiving forgiveness. This is not just so that God can teach us a lesson, but rather points to the need for our transformation in the process of forgiveness.

Discussion questions

Talking it through

1 In Psalm 51, verses 9 and 11, the psalmist desires personal sins to be removed from God's presence, but not to be personally removed from God. Is there a contradiction here? Can we be clearly separated from our sins or are they so deeply interrelated with our nature that we cannot be separated from them?

2 In what ways can we say with the psalmist that our sin is against God alone (Psalm 51, verse 4)? Is such a statement true?

3 To what does the psalmist refer in Psalm 51, verses 13 to 17 when speaking of God's salvation? What is its joy?

4 Psalm 51, verse 12 seems to imply that a life that knows God's forgiveness or salvation is a happy one. Do you agree that this is always the case? What sort of 'happiness' is to be understood here? Compare Matthew 5, verse 6.

Widening our horizons

1 Do you think some Christians focus on human sinfulness far too much to the detriment of their own and others' worth as loved and respected creatures before God? How do you think a healthy balance can be achieved?

2 At what point in our lives do you think we become responsible for our own sin?

3 In what ways can we prevent ourselves or others from experiencing God's forgiveness?

4 In wishing to share their experience of forgiveness, some people can become overbearing to others. In what ways can we 'teach transgressors [God's] ways' (verse 13) without ourselves becoming a hindrance to others experiencing God's mercy?

5 The psalmist seems to refer only to personal sins, but Psalm 51, verses 18 and 19 suggests the psalm can be applied to corporate sins as well. To what degree do we as individuals participate (even unconsciously) in the sins of our society? What are some of those sins?

You might consider such matters as society's attitude to ethnic minorities, the aid our country gives to other developing countries, unemployed people, migrants, and equality of the sexes and races.

Cultivating the practice of prayer

Have mercy on me, O God,
according to your steadfast love;
according to your abundant mercy
blot out my transgressions.

Psalm 51, verse 1

Meditate upon the mercy and steadfast love
of God which far surpasses our innate
human tendency to sin. Meditate on the
truth and wisdom that God desires within
us. Consider the joy of God's gift of salvation. Seek God's forgiveness for your own
sins. Seek God's forgiveness for those sins
in which we are all involved as part of our
society. Give thanks for the mercy of God,
for his continued presence with you, for his
sustaining you and restoring you.

O Lord, open my lips,
    and my mouth will declare your praise.

Psalm 51, verse 15

7
Psalms of trust and thanksgiving

I MENTIONED BEFORE THAT THE EXTREMES OF LIFE
are celebrated in Israel's psalms. The psalms move
back and forth between expressing anguish and joy.
The laments deal with anguish either as petition or
complaint. Psalms of trust or thanksgiving and
psalms of praise deal with joy.

An image of a world in which all the goodness
of creation is enjoyed and God is praised is what
shaped the faith of many Israelites. Zechariah 8,
verses 1 to 13 gives us a glimpse of this world in
which life is lived without tension, with orderliness,
goodness, reliability, prosperity and fertility. Evil is
punished and goodness is rewarded. This is *shalom*
— peace, prosperity and right relationships.

On the other side, the laments recognise that life can be thrown into chaos, beset by forces which oppress life and destroy it. Sometimes life can be seen as a conflict between the Lord — whose creative activity leads towards *shalom*, involving all aspects of covenant worship, justice, peace, fertility, prosperity, and right relationships with family, neighbours and God — and those forces of chaos which threaten these precious gifts: drought, enemy attack, injustice and enslavement.

In this context, the psalms of trust anticipate and the psalms of thanksgiving celebrate the establishment of an ordered life of *shalom*, recognising this order is a gift of God. So there is a connection between psalms of trust and thanksgiving on the one hand and psalms of lament on the other.[1] Psalms of trust are essentially an expansion of the trust elements which appear in the laments. Likewise, psalms of thanksgiving, which we do not have the space to deal with here, are an expansion of the praise elements in the laments.

PSALM 23: A psalm of trust

Psalm 23 is one of the best-known and most used of all psalms. It is a frequent choice for recitation at funerals and is one of the most used psalms in the lectionary readings in churches, occurring variously in the seasons of Lent, Easter and on the feast of Christ the King.

Because of its popularity, the readers of Psalm 23 have a familiarity with the text of the psalm which could not be assumed for any other psalm. However, that familiarity can easily lead readers either to assume too quickly that they have understood the psalm or to fail to read and appreciate it as closely as it deserves.

The psalm is full of metaphors, with those of the shepherd (verses 1 and 2) and the banquet table (verse 5) being the most prominent. The message of the psalm is conveyed primarily through imagery. There is no direct reference which enables us to catch a glimpse of the original setting of the psalm. This, coupled with the full use of metaphor, is why people over many generations have seen the psalm as fitting their particular circumstance.

The psalm breaks into three sections according to the way the Lord is addressed. The name 'Lord' appears only in verses 1 and 6, with the Lord being referred to in the third person, 'he' (verses 1 to 3 and 6). In verses 4 and 5, on the other hand, the Lord is addressed directly as 'you'. But even within these sections, the subject matter moves freely from one verse to another.

Peter Craigie notes that many scholars have broken the psalm up into two sections: verses 1 to 4 where the Lord is shepherd, and verses 5 to 6 where the Lord is host.[2] However, this division is not necessarily dictated by the content of the verses.[3]

It seems best to me to break the psalm along the lines of the way the Lord is addressed. Patrick Miller has referred to verse 4 as the centre of the psalm, calling it 'the gospel kernel of the Old Testament ... which itself echoes a word first given to the patriarchs and repeated again and again to Israel in moments of distress and fear: You don't have to be afraid'.[4]

Because it is impossible to place the psalm in a concrete setting and the many metaphors used in the psalm lend themselves to a great variety of situations, it is best not to ponder too much what the context of the writer might have been. It will be more profitable to see how the psalm works as a statement of trust.

❏ 'The Lord is my shepherd' (Psalm 23, verses 1 to 3) The psalm is clearly written from the 'sheep's point of view'. The use of the metaphor of shepherd for God is found elsewhere in the Old Testament — for example, in Genesis 49, verse 24; Isaiah 40, verse 11; Ezekiel 34, verses 11 to 16 (compare Psalm 80, verse 1, Psalm 95, verse 7 and Psalm 100, verse 3).

It is a metaphor found elsewhere in the ancient Near East — for example, in relation to the sun-god Shamash,[5] and in relation to the ideal picture of the Pharaoh of Egypt, of whom it is said:

He is the shepherd of all people; evil is not in his heart. Though his herds may be small, he has spent the day caring for them.[6]

The opening statement in Psalm 23 sums up the sense of trust and security in the Lord which the psalmist feels. The picture of the sheep, protected and guided by the shepherd, is extended through to verse 3. The sheep lies down in lush pasture, drinks from placid waters and is refreshed through the actions of the shepherd. The image of a sheep lying down under the protection of the shepherd is a symbol of security found in several places — for example, Ezekiel 34, verses 14 and 15 and Jeremiah 33, verse 12. It is also alluded to in Isaiah 14, verse 30.[7]

In these verses, there is a sense of complete dependence and confidence, with verse 3 summing this up with 'he restores my life'. The psalmist, as the sheep, has no need or want, all needs being seen to by the shepherd. We should note that the Hebrew expression for 'I shall not want' is rare in the Old Testament, occurring only here and in Nehemiah 9, verse 21. There, it is used in relation to the Lord's provision for his people as they journeyed through the wilderness after leaving Egypt. The sense of Israel 'lacking nothing' during the exodus is also present in Deuteronomy 2, verse 7.

The phrase in verse 3 translated variously as 'paths of righteousness' (RSV) or 'right paths' (NRSV) is ambiguous and, indeed, these two translations illustrate the problem. The ambiguity is in the Hebrew phrase itself, not just in the English translations. Does the phrase mean that the Lord leads the psalmist in ways of righteousness wherein the psalmist exercises justice and truth? Or does it mean that the Lord leads the psalmist in right paths which do not present the psalmist with personal obstacles or threats? This second meaning fits the rest of the psalm well.

On the other hand, the first sense cannot be completely ruled out. The phrase 'for his (your) name's sake', in reference to God, occurs several times in various psalms and prophetic books. It frequently accompanies a request for God's action in some matter or states that he has acted somehow.

When God acts, or is asked to act 'for his name's sake', it is usually in relation to God's own reputation, glory, righteousness or purpose.[8] Thus in the thinking of the psalmist, it is unlikely that the Lord's leading in secure, prosperous paths can be separated from the notion that they are also paths in which the psalmist will conform to the law of the Lord (see especially Psalm 25, verses 6 to 15).

❏ '. . .my cup overflows' (Psalm 23, verses 4 to 5)
In these verses, the psalmist addresses the Lord directly. Whereas in verses 1 to 3 the reader was told about a relationship, here the nature of that relationship is made all the more clear.

The psalmist reveals the intimacy of the relationship by indicating a lack of fear, the closeness of the Lord and the comfort he brings the psalmist. That

is contrasted with the fact that this closeness and
comfort is known in the most threating of places,
'the darkest valley' or 'the valley of the shadow of
death'.[9] Whatever the exact sense of the Hebrew,
which is not clear, the English reader does pick up
the notion that something ominous is being
described.

The same image of protection and provision in
the face of threat is carried on in verse 5. Again,
there is an element of ambiguity in the psalm. Is
the banquet which the Lord prepares for the psalmist
in the presence of the latter's enemies intended as
an image of provision and protection even in the
face of danger, or is it to be understood as a promise
of a victory feast over those who would oppose the
psalmist? The interpretation of a victory feast would
be appropriate if the psalm were intended to be said
by the king. The elements of anointing (verse 5)
and being lead in right paths (verse 3), if the latter
is understood in the sense of executing justice and
righteousness, would fit this context.

As a parallel to this, an ancient letter from the
city of Irqata in Lebanon to the Egyptian Pharaoh
and which was found at Tel El Amarna in Egypt,
says in part:

> May the king, our lord, heed the words of his
> loyal servants. May he grant a gift to his
> servants, so our enemies will see this and eat
> dirt (Letter No.100, lines 32–35).[10]

However, while there is no direct indication that the king was meant to be the speaker of the psalm, the points above can be understood easily in other ways. The simplest way to understand the imagery would seem to be to see in it a variety of metaphors which point to protection and provision in the broadest sense. This is supported by noting a similar expression in Psalm 78, verse 19. Psalm 78 is a history psalm and verses 17 to 20 recall part of Israel's wandering in the wilderness. In the context of the people grumbling at the hardship facing them, they ask: 'Can God spread a table in the wilderness?' While the presence of the enemies is lacking, the provision of God in times of hardship is clear.

❑ *'Surely goodness and mercy shall follow me. . .'* *(Psalm 23, verse 6)*

The psalm ends on a statement of sheer confidence. Goodness and mercy shall follow the psalmist who will dwell in the Lord's house for life. Such a statement could easily be understood as extremely presumptuous. Again, there is an element of ambiguity in the psalm. Whose goodness and mercy is mentioned? On whose or what authority does the psalmist claim to be in the presence of God continually?

However, the context of the whole psalm must be remembered. The psalmist has not known to this point any other confidence except that expressed in the Lord as provider and protector. The psalmist has no boast to make of his or her own righteousness. The psalmist stands silent and open before the Lord. In light of this, the goodness and mercy which follow the psalmist and the surety of the presence of the Lord can only be from the Lord himself.

The last verse, far from being a boast on the part of the psalmist, can be read as an extremely humbling statement about the goodness and mercy of the Lord which pursues the psalmist constantly — not to check on the psalmist's own goodness, but to bring comfort, provision, protection and joy. Such words are to be cherished and uttered with a sense of awe and reverence. Similar utterances can be found in other psalms such as Psalm 27, verses 4 to 6, Psalm 36, verses 7 to 9 and Psalm 52, verses 8 and 9.

❏ *The sense of Psalm 23*
A number of elements in the psalm seem to allude to the exodus wherein the Lord lead his people out of Egypt and through the wilderness. The image of the Lord leading his people like a shepherd is found in relation to the story of the exodus, or at least in an allusion to it, in a number of places (Psalm 80, verse 1; Psalm 77, verse 20 — both in the context of the first exodus; and in Ezekiel 34, verses 11 to 24; Isaiah 40, verse 11; Isaiah 49, verse 10 — in the context of the second exodus from Babylon to Jerusalem after exile).

The statement 'I shall not want' recalls, as we partly noted above, the lack of need while Israel was in the wilderness or in the land of conquest (Deuteronomy 2, verse 7; Deuteronomy 8, verse 9; and Nehemiah 9, verse 21).

The reference to the still waters could refer to the waters at Massah and Meribah (Exodus 17, verses 1 to 3). The guidance could be the exodus itself and the mercy (Hebrew: *hesed*, 'covenant loyalty') might refer to the covenant of Mt Sinai. The banquet table might pertain to the food provided in the wilderness or the covenant banquet described in Exodus 24, verse 11. The table prepared could also point to Israel's victory over its enemies and, finally, the house of the Lord could refer to the promised land itself. Exodus 15 contains a poem which ends in verse 18 with the Lord declared king. In verse 17, the land of promise is described as the Lord's sanctuary.

Following this line of thinking, Psalm 23 could be intended to allude to the exodus event. The individual in the psalm could be a personification of the whole community. If the psalm has a late exilic origin, then the call to trust could be for the Israelites in exile to have confidence and undertake a 'second exodus' back to the promised land.

David Freedman has commented on the influence exodus imagery has had on the psalm, but sees the purpose differently:

. . .the poet wishes to evoke the past, especially
the wilderness experience, but not to dwell on
it. His main interest is elsewhere: to use the
past as a key to the present and the future,
and to express his conviction that the God who
was shepherd to his people in the ancient past —
and led them through the wilderness to freedom,
security and peace — would and will do the
same and more for his people now and in the future. The message is conveyed by an individual
to other individuals: each member of the community is a bearer of the tradition, a recipient of
the blessing and the promise which inhere in it.[11]

But this interpretation in terms of the exodus is
by no means the only way the psalm can be read,
as we have already indicated. The scholar Artur
Weiser has seen the psalm marked by the 'tender
touch of a serene soul enjoying perfect peace of mind
which comes from trust in God'.[12] The psalm gives
a picture of the mature trust of one who:

. . .having passed through bitter experiences of
having fought many battles (verses 4 and 5), had
been allowed to find at the decline of life in its
intimate communion with God (verses 2 and 6)
the serenity of a contented spirit — peace of
mind (verse 6) and, in all dangers, strength.[13]

For Weiser, the occasion of the psalm is an experience of the psalmist during worship which

brought home 'happiness and blessing of communion with God'.[14] In this vein, Jews and Christians have used the psalm as both a prayer of comfort and a prayer of thanksgiving for strength in time of difficulty.

But Psalm 23 ought not to be seen as an example of sentimental piety. As Claus Westermann notes in a word of caution on the psalm:

> The twenty-third Psalm, the best-known of all the psalms, is often viewed as an idyll — as a cheerful, ideal picture of a quite unreal relationship with God. That it is not and that it never was.[15]

While we might tend to romanticise the image of the shepherd in our use of the psalm, the dangers faced in the lives of shepherds in the ancient world were real. If the shepherd imagery is drawn from the language used of the king, then the enemies referred to are no less real. The calming, confident words of the psalm are intended to meet the real anxieties, fears and hopes of people of every standing in life. The words of the psalm are not to be taken lightly, nor are the situations which those words address.

But more can be noted. The words of the psalm are not just offered as words to soothe the troubled mind. The psalm is not just a general expression of trust. It is an expression of trust *in the Lord*. As we noted above, the name 'Lord' forms an envelope to

the psalm, being used in the first and last verses
only. This could be seen as a kind of literary device
pointing us to the fact that the Lord is the beginning
and the end of our trust, the one who shields us
round about with his goodness, mercy and
provision.

To say the words of the psalm is then not just to
utter words of comfort, but it is to engage in a level
of reality that goes beyond the level of any threat
to our well-being. Claus Westermann puts it this
way:

> What the psalm says is this: when a man in all
> that he experiences in life seizes hold of trust —
> whether he is worrying about his daily bread,
> asking after the right path or feeling himself in
> deadly peril — when he trusts that he will be
> upheld, that there is someone who takes care of
> him, then in and through that trust he has
> achieved fellowship with God and he can say
> 'God is my shepherd'.[16]

Other psalms of trust and thanksgiving

(a) Psalm 131 focuses on one central image of trust.
What is it? What does it add to our understanding
of the nature of trust in God? Artur Weiser has
remarked on this psalm that:

> . . .the [psalmist's] soul rests on God's heart and
> finds its happiness in intimate communion with

him, not like an infant crying loudly for its mother's breast, but like a weaned child that quietly rests by its mother's side, happy in being with her.[17]

(b) *Psalm 121* is often called the 'traveller's psalm'. It pictures a pilgrim doing one of two things: either setting out on a pilgrimage to Jerusalem and having anxieties for the journey calmed; or, renewed by the festival worship, looking to the holy hill and being reminded of the Lord's help as he or she returns to the workaday world.

Note that the speaker in the psalm changes between verses 2 and 3. In verses 1 and 2, the pilgrim speaks, but in verses 3 to 8 the pilgrim is spoken to. The point of the psalm is that the Lord's protection and preservation of the pilgrim — and Israel — is never ceasing, invading all areas of life.

(c) *Psalm 107* is a good example of a community psalm of thanksgiving. Note the regular structure of this psalm, with the four different groups of people mentioned in verses 4 to 32 and the refrains that occur in each section.

In verses 33 to 38, the psalm states that the Lord is the one who controls creation. He does good and brings evil in judgment. It is thus a psalm which looks back and celebrates the survival of various people in times of trouble because of their trust in the Lord.

It ends with the Lord's people expressing their

trust that he can restore them when they again find themselves in dire straits; and it calls the Lord's people to rejoice in his deliverance — to consider 'these things' and the Lord's faithful acts.

Discussion questions

 Talking it through

1 Can you recall some situation, whether formal or informal, where Psalm 23 was used with telling effect? Explain *why* you felt the psalm spoke with such power on this occasion. Was it just the familiarity of the words or was it something deeper?

2 Note the ways Psalm 23 has been interpreted above (pages 150 to 152). St Augustine (AD 354–430) interpreted the psalm as an address by the church to Christ. Martin Luther (1483–1546) saw the psalm as having to do with the comfort of the individual Christian who hears and understands that the word of God is scripture.

Do you think their interpretations are appropriate or not? What to you is the key purpose of the psalm?

3 What type of person do you think could have written this psalm:

a shepherd?

a king?

a professional hymn-writer?

a peasant?

a wealthy land owner?

What differences does it make to how you understand the psalm if you imagine these different people writing it?

Widening our horizons

1 As you read or hear Psalm 23 again, what images come into your mind? Do these images enhance your appreciation in a way that words alone cannot? How do you think God uses the gift of images?

2 What situations in the modern world shatter the trust of various people in:

their relatives?
the people they work with?
schoolfriends?
society?
government?
the police and justice system?
the church?

Who are some of those people who have lost trust, do you think? Is this loss of faith ever:

(a) understandable?
(b) justifiable?

3 Why is it so difficult in modern society for people to trust in God? Do you believe it was any easier in the days when Psalm 23 was first written?

Be realistic: What changes in contemporary society have 'loaded the dice' against a full-orbed, open-hearted faith in God? By contrast, what particular elements in modern life make it conducive again to believe?

4 In what ways is trust in other people related to trust in God? In what ways can those of us who are in a position of trust affirm and build up others' faith in God? Similarly, how can we undermine that trust, whether intentionally or unintentionally?

Why does penitence — being prepared to confess our sin and change the direction of our life — have a positive affect on our relationship with God?

5 Does God's goodness and mercy to his people mean that they will always be comfortable and well-off financially, in bodily or mental health, satisfied with work, with a sense of fulfilment in their lives? If not, what is meant, then, by 'God's goodness and mercy'?

Cultivating the practice of prayer

The Lord is my shepherd,
I shall not want.

Psalm 23, verse 1

Meditate on the times when you have been
restored, led in right paths, or comforted in
times of distress or fear. Consider the goodness of the Lord to you, your community,
our nation and our world. Give thanks to
God for his comfort in times when you
have personally known his presence and
when he has comforted you through others.
Pray for those who need God's comfort,
protection and provision: those known to
you by name; those suffering within our
society; those in far-off places torn by war,
oppression or natural disaster. Give thanks
to God for his faithfulness to all people.

Surely goodness and mercy shall follow me
all the days of my life,
and I shall dwell in the house of the Lord
my whole life long.

Psalm 23, verse 6

8
Psalms of enthronement

❧

THERE ARE TWO CATEGORIES of royal psalms: those that celebrate the Lord as king (*enthronement* psalms) and those that refer to human kingship (*royal* psalms). We will mention some of this latter group briefly at the end of the chapter.

Psalms celebrating God's enthronement
Many of the psalms in this category begin with the Hebrew clause *yahweh malak*, which can be translated either as 'the Lord is king' or 'the Lord has become king'. Psalms in this group include Psalms 29, 47, 93 and 96 to 99. They are all psalms of praise to the Lord.

Enthronement psalms have two features. The

first concerns the relationship between kingship and creation in ancient Israel. Enthronement psalms celebrate the kingship of the Lord, shown in the Lord's power over the forces of chaos. When we looked earlier at the creation psalms, we saw that creation stories in the Ancient Near East often involved a struggle between the creator god, who brought fertility and life to the earth, and forces of chaos or sterility, often represented as a monster. They would end with a celebration of the sovereignty and majesty of the creator god.

Enthronement psalms fit in with this pattern of celebration. In the Ancient Near East, the concepts of creation and kingship are inseparable.

The concept of the kingship of God in Israel is a very ancient idea. It could well date back to a time before the adoption of human kingship as a form of social organisation and government. The poem in Exodus 15 sees the Lord's deliverance of his people from Egypt as the very basis for the celebration of the kingship of Israel's God (see especially verse 18).[1] While the poem does not specifically mention God as creator, the victory of God over the army of Pharaoh at the sea (mentioned in verses 4 to 10) contains echoes of the victory of the creator God over the forces of chaos, represented as a sea monster. In Israel, the kingship of God is associated with the notions of God as both creator and redeemer.

The second feature of enthronement psalms is

that they draw on the metaphor of 'kingship' to speak about divine power and authority. This is not only a royal, but a political metaphor. As a metaphor, it has its limitations as well as its benefits. To use this metaphor to speak about God brings into focus the way power should be exercised within the community. When the people of Israel first wanted a human king to lead them, the major question raised by the prophet Samuel was how this human kingship would relate to the kingship of God over his people?[2]

To maintain a belief in the kingship or supreme power of God means that all other powers must be seen in relation to that power. They are all judged by that power, whether they be political or judicial powers — or the kind of personal power we exercise in determining the direction and activities of our own lives. Walter Brueggemann has remarked:

> That [the Lord] is a royal power serves to destabilise every other royal power, to relativise every temptation to absolutise power. This kingship is a gift of freedom, for allegiance to this liberating God tells against every other political subservience. . .[3]

To celebrate and praise God as king means to acknowledge God's authority and responsibility — to be answerable to God. It is also, by implication, to acknowledge the limitations of one's own life.

The setting in which the enthronement psalms were used is not entirely clear. One major proposal has been made by Sigmund Mowinckel, whom we mentioned briefly in chapter 1. He proposed that a festival for the enthronement of the Lord could have been celebrated in Israelite worship. He based his argument on an interpretation of the phrase *yahweh malak*. He understood it to mean '[the Lord] has become king' — that is, the Lord has been enthroned. This festival, according to Mowinckel, would have been celebrated every year, possibly in an autumn New Year festival in Jerusalem.[4]

Mowinckel drew on the analogy of a Babylonian New Year festival, called the *akitu* festival, in his proposal. In the *akitu* festival, the kingship of the Babylonian god Marduk was celebrated. The festival recalled the cycles of nature. It was a celebration of fertility over sterility. Marduk's kingship guaranteed the former. During the festival, there was the recital of the Babylonian creation epic *Enuma Elish*, which recalled the victory of the storm god Marduk over chaos.

The festival was held at the beginning of the new agricultural year. Human celebrants, especially the king, participated in a re-enactment of the heavenly drama of life over death, a celebration which was thought to make the earth fertile rather than sterile.[5]

Many scholars today would accept the proposal of an autumn New Year festival in Israel celebrating the Lord's kingship. It is suggested by some that this festival developed into the later Festival of Booths.[6] It has been proposed that the Israelite king took part in the festival and that the enthronement psalms featured in the liturgy.[7]

Nevertheless, while the proposal is widely accepted in one form or another, there are some well-recognised problems with it. These focus on the time of year when the festival may have been celebrated, the lack of any clear evidence in the Old Testament for the festival, and the fact that the clause *yahweh malak* does not demand an enthronement liturgy. However, even those scholars who remain sceptical about the existence of a special enthronement festival in ancient Israel still accept that the kingship of God was probably celebrated on occasion in Israel — as Psalms 24 and 132 imply.

PSALM 93: A psalm celebrating God's enthronment

Psalm 93 falls into three sections: verses 1 and 2; verses 3 and 4; and verse 5.

The first section (verses 1 and 2) begins, as do other enthronement psalms, with the statement *yahweh malak*, translated in the NRSV as 'The Lord is king!' These verses paint a clear picture of the Lord as monarch, robed in his regal attire of majesty and strength. The section concludes with a statement of the eternal nature of the Lord's enthronement. Both he and his reign have been from time immemorial. Sandwiched in the middle of this initial section is a statement that the Lord has established the world and that it will never be moved.

In this initial statement of the kingship of the Lord, there is a clear example of the connection between divine kingship and creation. The creation of the world is itself support for the statement that the Lord is king. Creation is a clear demonstration of the reality of kingship. Further, creation, like the Lord himself and his kingship, is eternal. Therefore, to speak about the Lord as king is to speak about the order of the world and its life. To affirm that the Lord is king is to state that he has the world under control. There is order and a rationality to life. In proclaiming the Lord as king, the people are meant to feel 'comfortable' in the world and have a confidence in life.

The second section of the psalm (verses 3 and 4) opens up the other side of this issue. Life is threatened by powers of chaos in many forms. This leads variously to uncertainty, illness, distress and insecurity. The affirmation that the Lord is king is a statement that those powers cannot prevail. The Lord is mightier.

The image at the heart of this second section is taken from a tradition in Israel which has a lot in common with creation mythology in the Ancient Near East. The Hebrew in verse 3 refers to the

'rivers' — 'ocean depths' (GNB) or 'seas' (NIV) —
which have raised their voices. The NRSV translates
this as 'the floods' and, in so doing, captures the
essence of the imagery. Verse 3 is not speaking
about rivers in the mundane, earthly sense, but is
talking about the cosmic waters, those which are
pushed aside to make way for the creation of the
cosmos (compare Genesis 1, verses 6 to 8). In
Canaanite mythology, the god Yamm, against whom
Baal fights in order to become king over all the earth,
is called 'Prince Sea, Judge River'. Moreover, in
verse 4 the Hebrew phrase *mayim rabbim*, translated
as 'mighty waters', is usually used to refer to the
cosmic waters.

Thus, in this psalm about kingship, we have
further reference to creation (verses 3 and 4). This
time, however, creation is referred to in such a way
as to emphasise it is the Lord's majesty which puts
aside all that is chaos — all that leads to alienation
and disruption. We should note that while the
Hebrew terms translated 'majesty' or 'majestic' in
the NRSV (verses 1 and 4 respectively) are not related,
the two verses are meant to represent two sides of
the one coin. The majesty associated with the Lord
in extolling his kingship over creation is that same
majesty which sets at rest those forces which challenge his kingship.

This brief psalm concludes with verse 5, which
brings the scene down to earth. Here, we find the

psalmist speaking about decrees and about the Temple. The Law and the Temple are institutions firmly fixed in the everyday worship of the community of faithful Israelites. The psalmist proclaims that the decrees are firm and that holiness is befitting to the Lord's house for evermore.

These two scenes — creation and divine kingship, and the worshipping life of the ordinary Israelite — may seem to be quite different on the surface, but the two are by no means separate worlds. The Law is given, as we saw in relation to the *torah* psalms, so that divine order can be established within the world which has been created. In other words, it is given so that the divine ordering of life in creation can be continued in the daily living of the faithful community. The Temple located in Jerusalem was intended to be an exact replica of the heavenly home of the Lord. Thus, both the earthly Temple and the Law have their cosmic counterparts and connections.

Moreover, we should note that the Law and the Temple are respectively immovable and eternal in nature. These are appropriate qualities of a world created by the Lord and of the Lord's kingship itself. In other words, the eternal nature of the Lord's kingship, described vividly in both positive and negative terms in verses 1 to 4, is now to be seen in the Law and the presence of the Temple in the midst of the people.

When the Lord is proclaimed king in Psalm 93

and in other psalms, it is part of a statement of trust
and confidence that he will provide peace, security
and order in the world. In Jewish tradition and in
the Mishnah, Psalm 93 is sung at the beginning of
Sabbath, the day of rest. In Genesis 2, verse 2, we
are told God rested after creating the earth. That
rest is a sign of his rule over the creation, a rule
which intends to bring a lasting and good peace.

PSALM 99: A psalm celebrating God's sovereignty

The very structure of this psalm seems to suggest
ways it might have been used as part of a liturgy
in ancient Israel. The psalm keeps alternating between statements about the Lord and the people,
statements made directly to the Lord and other statements which could be uttered by the people
themselves. The psalm thus seems to be a three-way
dialogue between a worship leader (speaking for the
psalmist), the people and the Lord.

However, as will be seen below, it is not always
clear who is speaking to whom. The psalm is a
good illustration of the difficulty involved in trying
to reconstruct the ancient setting of the psalms.

Verses 1 and 2 contain third person statements
about the kingship of the Lord. As is the case of
Psalm 93, this psalm begins with the brief exclamation *yahweh malak*, 'The Lord is king!' The kingship
of the Lord is then related to the peoples of the

earth. They are called to tremble even as the earth quakes at the enthronement of the Lord. In the psalm, we see that the Lord is described as universal sovereign, but in a special way he is also sovereign to his people (verse 3).

There is a specificity in this psalm as in other enthronement psalms which we cannot escape. The Lord is always proclaimed king in relation to *someone*. That someone is usually Israel. So just as lament psalms are willing to name the enemies of the Lord, so the enthronement psalms name those who acknowledge the Lord as king. The kingship of the Lord is evident in specific human instances of justice, equity and righteousness. His kingship over other nations in the world proceeds from that point.

The reference to the Lord being 'enthroned upon the cherubim' (verse 1) could allude to the ark of the covenant, which had two carved cherubim on top and possibly represented the throne of the Lord. In Ancient Near Eastern engravings and relief sculptures, cherubim were often pictured as the arms of a divine throne.

In verse 3, the psalmist tells the Lord that the people should praise his name. It is followed by the refrain, 'Holy is he!' Note that this refrain is repeated at the end of verse 5 and a fuller statement that the Lord is holy concludes the psalm in verse 9. The beginning of verse 5 is almost the same as the beginning of verse 9. It is difficult to know who utters this refrain. One possibility is that it is said by all the people as a response to the injunction of a leader. Alternatively, the statement at the end of verse 3 could be made by the leader of worship as part of the injunction for the people to praise the Lord. This is less likely if verses 5 and 9 are taken into account because, in each of those cases, the whole verse is addressed to the people.

The presence of the refrain suggests a three-fold structure to the psalm. The content of the psalm falls into three distinct sections around the refrain. The first section contains an exclamation that the Lord is king in Zion and over the nations. Within each section, however, the changes of addressee, or possibly even speaker, continue.

Verses 4 and 5 constitute the second section of the psalm. It is not absolutely clear in verse 4 whom the psalmist is addressing. It could be an address to the Lord or, alternatively, to the earthly king. It is my opinion that the Lord is being addressed in verse 4 as this fits in with the reference to the kingship of the Lord in verse 1.

If the earthly king were being addressed in verse 4, it is difficult to see why the people should be called on to extoll the Lord in verse 5.[8] If the assumption that the Lord is addressed in verse 4 is correct, then he is seen as a lover of justice, an establisher of equity and a doer of righteousness.

Thus after the first section, in which the kingship of the Lord is exclaimed, this section outlines what that kingship entails. The Lord fulfils his royal role fully.[9]

Verses 6 to 9 make up the third and longest section of the psalm. In verses 6 and 7, the Lord is referred to again in the third person. Reference is made to Moses, Aaron and Samuel as examples of those who had cried to the Lord and whom he had answered. Stress is not only put on the Lord's attitude towards them, but on their faithful attitude towards him (verse 7). While there is the assurance that a cry to the Lord will be met by the deliverance of the Lord, it needs to be recognised that the other side of that is obedience to the Lord's law — 'they kept his decree' (verse 7).

Thus the kingship of the Lord is seen both in his attentive response to his people *and* in the requirement of an attentive response by the people towards him. There is a dual expectation of the divine presence with the people and of obedience by the people to the divine will. Divine presence and obedience to the divine will both involve justice, equity and righteousness.

The third section finishes with an extended address to the Lord (verse 8) in which he is portrayed as both one who forgives his people and as one who avenges the wrongs done by them. There follows an injunction for the people to praise the Lord (verse 9). It is clear that the leader of worship speaks throughout this verse. This section, following the exclamation of the Lord as king and then the statement of what that kingship entails, provides a specific set of examples from Israel's past of a proper response to that kingship and the result that response brings.

So the one who proclaims *yahweh malak* (verse 1) should do so in full awareness of what a proper relationship with the Lord entails. The people who praise the holiness of the Lord should know that the holiness to be praised involves a certain divine freedom which does not suffer human manipulation.

Psalms referring to a human king

The collection of royal psalms includes Psalms 2, 18, 20, 21, 45, 72, 89, 101, 110 and 144 (verses 1 to 11). They cover various aspects of the royal life, including coronation (Psalm 2) and even a royal wedding (Psalm 45).

I will deal here briefly with two royal psalms.

PSALM 2: A psalm of enthronement

Psalm 2 was apparently associated with the enthronement of the human king in Jerusalem. This is evident in verses 6 to 7 where the Lord declares that he has set his king in Zion.

Verse 7 clearly indicates that when a king was enthroned, he was regarded as 'the son' of the Lord. This verse was later read by New Testament writers as the statement of God about Jesus who is God's 'son' in a new sense (see Acts 13, verse 33, Hebrews 1, verse 5 and Hebrews 5, verse 5).

Psalm 2 begins by speaking about the nations who conspire against the Lord and his king. The Lord's response is to laugh at this opposition and threaten them (verse 5). The Lord is king in heaven and he sets his own king in Jerusalem. Kingship in Israel is tied closely to the concept of the Lord as king over the cosmos. The human king's desire to be sovereign on earth will be fulfilled by the Lord and is based in the sovereignty of the Lord over all creation. Compare verse 9 with verse 5.

The last section of the psalm, verses 10 and 11, returns to the scene of the kings of the nations. It contains a warning to them to give allegiance to the one who is sovereign over all.

This psalm has some military overtones that may not sit easily with a Christian commitment to peace and reconciliation. We need to recognise that the psalm comes from another time and place. While we may not want to embrace what it says literally, nor even share some of the vehemence of its sentiment, the question of the sovereignty of the Lord over the creation is the key point here for us.

A commitment to a God who is love, and who desires justice and freedom for all peoples, will inevitably lead to confrontation with forces which seek to destroy those things. While violence is an extremely limited option for a Christian, if one at all, confrontation of evil in many forms should not and cannot be avoided.

PSALM 72: A psalm of human kingship

In this psalm, the human king is seen as the recipient of the justice and righteousness of the divine king. The human king is a trustee of the divine royal way. Continuity of order in the world is set up by the Lord and is conveyed through the political structures.

Three requests for the human king are made throughout the psalm. The first is that the king may put into practice the righteousness and justice that are the foundation of the Lord's kingship (verses 4, and 12 to 14). The second is that the human king may live long and be to his people like the rain that falls on the mown grass and the showers that water the earth (verse 6) — that is, may he bring prosperity and peace. The third request is that he may have dominion over the world and his foes (verses 8 to 11). Here is the military and political aspect of kingship.

In the psalm, the three elements of social justice, prosperity and political-military security are tied together.

Discussion questions

Talking it through

1 In enthronement and royal psalms social justice, prosperity and political-military security are closely linked. What is meant by 'prosperity' in these psalms?

2 The title 'king' carries with it patriarchal or sexist overtones for many people. Others might see it as suggestive of a tyrannical rule. Still others may see it as a title portraying a position without any real authority.

   What other titles or images might better portray for you God's authority and position in relation to creation, society and you as an individual?

3 Psalm 99, verses 6 and 7 recall heroes from Israel's past history who have cried out to the Lord and who have been faithful. What biblical heroes or heroines, other than the ones mentioned, could be recalled here?

Widening our horizons

1 In ancient Israel, the relationship between human kingship and the kingship of God was an issue that had to be addressed many times. In recent centuries in Western nations, this same issue has appeared in the guise of the struggle between 'church' and 'state'.

(a) At what points do you believe there is a degree of *harmony* in giving allegiance to both God and our nation, and at what points is there *tension*? Can you give an example of each?

(b) How do you decide when to 'render to Caesar the things that are Caesar's and to God the things that are God's' (Matthew 22, verse 21)?

2 Does the way we live and the worship we offer reflect the sovereignty of God over all creation? In what ways can this be strengthened? How can we practically express the idea of *yahweh malak*, 'the Lord is king!'

3 You may have noted, as we've studied this book, that the psalms keep raising the question of how God's good intent in creation lies at odds with human experience of suffering in the world.

(a) Have you had any further thoughts on this issue? Has your study of the psalms helped you understand this perennial problem any better?

(b) Can God's good intent for his world and the presence of suffering ever be reconciled? If not, how are we meant to live with this conflict? Compare Romans 8, verses 38 and 39.

4 Who are the heroes or heroines of faith in your community whose lives have given honour to God and who have been models of faithfulness for others?

5 Do you think the issues of social justice, prosperity and political-military security are or should be as closely linked in our world today as they were in Israel? Should there be more awareness of a relationship between them?

Cultivating the practice of prayer

O sing to the Lord a new song,
for he has done marvellous things.
His right hand and his holy arm
have gotten him victory.

Psalm 98, verse 1

Meditate on the marvellous things God has
done for you, for your community, and in
creation at large. Consider how he has been
faithful to his creation. Give praise to God
in some new way.
Imagine your praise joining with the praise
of the whole creation. Consider every part
of your life this day an act of praise to God.

Let the sea roar, and all that fills it;
the world and those who live in it.
Let the floods clap their hands;
let the hills sing together for joy
at the presence of the Lord, for he is
coming to judge the earth.
He will judge the world with righteousness,
and the peoples with equity.

Psalm 98, verses 7 to 9

9
Psalms of praise

'THE SOVEREIGNTY OF GOD is given language and structure' in the psalms of praise, says Patrick Miller:

> There the majesty and power of the Lord are uncovered and made visible. In the hymns of Israel the most elemental structure of Old Testament faith is set forth. . . In what is said, we learn of the one we call Lord. In the way it is said — in both shape and tone — we are given a model for our own response to God. . . Praise is language to God and about God, elicited out of human experience.[1]

Claus Westermann has argued that psalms of praise constitute one pole on a continuum in the collection of psalms in the Bible. That continuum ranges between *supplication* on the one hand and *praise* on the other.[2]

Other scholars recognise this movement between

extremes, but describe it in slightly different ways. For example, C.C. Broyles sees the extremes as being *complaint* (rather than supplication) and *praise*.[3]

However, this understanding of the psalms needs to be qualified. Praise is not just one end of the continuum, nor do the psalms simply move back and forth between lament and praise. Rather, praise is at the very heart of faith and hence features prominently in the psalms as a whole. One always moves towards praise. It is the final word, not just one end of a continuum.

The Book of Psalms actually reflects this in that, while laments dominate in the first half, hymns of praise dominate in the second half of the Book. The movement is not one directional by any means, but the trend is in that direction. The whole Book of Psalms ends with a series of hymns of praise (Psalms 146 to 150). Even the final Hebrew word in the book is *hallelujah*, 'Praise the Lord'.

This has been noted by several scholars.[4] Patrick Miller writes:

To go through the Book of Psalms is to be led increasingly towards the praise of God as the final word. While doxology *may* be the beginning word, it *is* clearly the *final* word. That is so *theologically*, because in praise more than in any other human act, God is seen and declared to be God in all fullness and glory. That is so *eschatologically*, in that the last word of all is the

confession and praise of God by the whole
creation. And that is so *for the life of faith*,
because praise, more than any other act, fully
expresses utter devotion to God and the loss of
self in extravagant exaltation of the transcendent
Lord who is the ground of all.[5]

Thus praise is a response to people's experience
of God's grace and power. In the Old Testament,
according to Miller's quote above, praise is both
theology (it tells about God) and *testimony for conver-
sion* (it seeks to draw others into the circle of
worshippers).[6]

The form and content of the psalms of praise

The point that praise is both theology and testimony
is seen clearly in the form and content of the psalms
of praise. As an example of the structure of those
psalms, we will take Psalm 117, the shortest psalm
of all.

The structure in this psalm is very simple, but it
illustrates the general structure in all these psalms.
It begins with a *summons* or a *call to praise* (verse 1).
Other hymns could have a declaration of praise or
both a call and declaration. The psalm then ends
with a *reason for praise* (verse 2). This reason is fairly
general in content. The sentiment expressed can also
be found in the part of the hymn quoted in Exodus
34, verse 6.

Note that in the case of Psalm 117 a further brief call to praise concludes the psalm.

This structure is also seen in hymns outside the Book of Psalms. For example, it is evident in Exodus 15, verse 21, known as the 'Song of Miriam' and sung as the Lord delivered Israel at the Red Sea. This brief hymn, which may have been a summary of a much longer hymn (compare Exodus 15, verses 1 to 18), has the structure:

> Sing to the Lord (*call to praise*), for he has triumphed gloriously;
> the horse and his rider he has thrown into the sea (*reason for praise*).

It should be noted that the reason for praise can appear in different forms in different psalms. Claus Westermann has made the distinction within the general category of hymns of praise between psalms of *declarative praise* — where the reason for the praise is some specific past deed which God has done for his people (Exodus 15, verse 21) — and psalms of *descriptive praise* — in which the reason for praise is God's action in general or his nature (Psalm 117).

Finally, we should note that hymns of praise also include some of the psalms studied earlier — for example, the psalms of creation and history.

The imaginative element in the psalms of praise

Walter Brueggemann has argued that the praise of God is not just a responsive activity, but what he calls a constitutive one. On the one hand, the offering of praise can arise as a response to some past action of God or to the nature of God. But it can be more than that.

When an act of praise is offered, it can also invite the participant to enter into a new experience which is unrelated or goes beyond their past experience. It can invite the participant to imagine how different things could be to the present. When people praise God, they imagine the glory of God and exalt God above all else. Such can happen as a way of giving thanks to God or as a way of imagining how you would like things to be under the charge of God in his glory. Brueggemann concludes:

> Praise is not a response to a world already fixed and settled, but it is a responsive and obedient participation in a world yet to be decreed and in process of being decreed through this liturgical act.[8]

But there are dangers in this. Praise can be used to give people false hopes. It can be manipulated to give people the impression that God *will* do things for them and their present, perhaps painful circumstances can be set aside.

This is especially important for those who are called to lead in the liturgy or worship. They need to consider carefully the world they create for their people and the God they characterise in their worship. This is particularly the case with praise.

If there is too much praise in worship without just reason for it, it can create a picture of a God who has little to do with the sufferings of the people. If praise is offered for its own sake without concern for what is happening in the life of the community, it can create hurt and a feeling in some of being cut off from God.

PSALM 150: A psalm of praise

Psalm 150 not only brings us to the end of the Book of Psalms, but concludes the collection of hymns of praise found in Psalms 146 to 150. Each of Psalms 146 to 149 begin and end with the imperative *hallelujah*, 'Praise the Lord!' Psalm 150 has often been considered as the concluding doxology to the Book of Psalms, performing a similar task to the doxologies at the end of each of the first four books of psalms.

In Westermann's terminology noted above, Psalm 150 would be a psalm of descriptive praise. After the call to praise the Lord, verse 1 calls for the Lord to be praised in his sanctuary and in his mighty firmament. The word 'firmament', in Hebrew *raqia^c*, is the same term used in the creation story in Genesis

1, verse 6 — translated in the NRSV as 'dome'. It
means the sky or heavens. The sense of verse 1 is,
then, to call on all who worship the Lord both in
his earthly sanctuary and in the heavenly realm to
praise him. This reminds us of the part in the prayer
of thanksgiving in the communion service where the
minister says something like: 'And so we praise
you with the faithful of every time and place, joining
with choirs of angels and the whole creation in the
eternal hymn. . .'

The congregation responds with the words of
praise: 'Holy, holy, holy Lord, God of power and
might'.

Verse 2 continues to call for the Lord to be
praised, but also incorporates the reasons for praise
into the summons. Both the mighty deeds of the
Lord and his own greatness are cited. The deeds
are not specified but, given the position of the psalm,
we can assume that all of the deeds of the Lord are
indicated.

The central section of the psalm (verses 3 to 5)
gives a brief catalogue of the ways the worshippers
are to praise the Lord. Apart from the reference to
dancing in verse 4, we have here a list of musical
instruments. These could well have been the ones
used in worship in ancient Israel. The NSRV lists
them as trumpet, lute, harp, tambourine, stringed
instruments, pipe and cymbals. While we read of
most of these instruments elsewhere in the Old Tes-

tament and we have an idea of how some of them looked from pictures discovered in archaeological finds, the exact nature of some of them is not clear and how they were played and sounded remains a puzzle.

The interesting thing about these verses is that they call upon the people to praise the Lord in ways that do not involve words. Our own praise in hymns and music usually involves words. It may be that the psalms were sung to the accompaniment of one or more of these instruments, but this psalm does not stress that. What it does promote is that the praise of the Lord can be effected by the playing of music and by dance. In other words, it suggests to us ways of praising God without words. This is praise that comes from the feelings, not only the mind.

Throughout this section, and even in verses 1 and 2 and the beginning of verse 6, a rhythm is set up. Each half line begins with the Hebrew word *halleluhu*, 'praise him'. A chant is thus created with only the last part of each half line differing. This chant may well have been intended to go with the playing of the instruments mentioned in the psalm.

Finally, the psalm concludes with two half-lines which break the pattern set up in the previous verses. These lines do not begin with the familiar *halleluhu*. They do, however, conclude with the divine name *Yah*, a shortened version of *Yahweh*. In

verse 6, there is the desire that everything that
breathes might praise the Lord. It may be that not
only the worshippers in the sanctuary and in the
heavens are called upon to praise, but that the
psalmist imagines all creatures giving praise to the
Lord. Their very life, and the living of it, is that
which praises the Lord.

Psalm 150 invites us to explore new opportunities
for praise. However, Walter Brueggemann sees this
psalm as the one which is most open to abuse. It
is a pure summons to praise with little reason given
for the praise. Because there is no real description
of who this Lord is that is praised, there is the danger
that, in using this psalm, praise can be offered
without any thought as to how the Lord relates to
the world in which the worshipper lives.[9] In other
words, this psalm could be used in any context from
those where the Lord is preached as a tyrannical
God to those where the justice and care of God for
the poor is paramount in the minds of the people.

While the potential misuse of this psalm is real,
Brueggemann's caution about its use may be too
hasty. Certainly one should not sing this total summons
to praise too quickly, but the reason for praise is not
just supplied by the words of a psalm. It can be
hidden in the unstated experience of the people.
Words alone do not create worlds.

So while we need to be careful how we use a
psalm such as this, we should still use it! Its sheer

exuberance in inviting us to praise God in ways that move beyond the limitations of our thoughts and words is what should capture our attention.

Leslie Allen concludes his comments on Psalm 150 with these words:

> The one-sidedness of this hymn of praise, as a series of summonses without the corresponding grounds for praise, gives a fascinating open-ended effect to the psalm. If all who hear and all who read it are drawn to fill their hearts with a conviction of God's praiseworthiness and to answer these strenuous calls to worship with equally fervent praise, this psalm will have accomplished its noble aim.[10]

Other psalms of praise

As noted above, some hymns also fall into the categories of psalms about creation or history psalms. Some of the psalms following may seem as though they belong in other categories as well as here.

(a) Psalm 100 calls for a joyful noise and singing to be made to the Lord in a way similar to the call in Psalm 150 for music-making and dancing. The reason for praise here is that the Lord has 'created' Israel (verse 3). Verse 4 invites thanksgiving to the Lord.

The relation of thanksgiving psalms to hymns of

praise is close. Verse 5 concludes with echoes of other psalms of praise. Compare Psalm 117, verse 2.

(b) *Psalm 113* also begins and ends with *hallelujah*. The summons to praise invites the people to praise the Lord's name. It is blessed eternally (verse 2) and so the worshippers are called to praise the name of the Lord every waking hour (verse 3).

The reason for praise begins in verse 4. The psalm focuses on the majesty of the Lord who is pictured as high above all. But then a contrast is created in verses 7 to 9. The majesty of the Lord, while in and of itself worthy of praise, is seen in the way the Lord on high exalts those who are lowly on the earth to positions of honour (compare 1 Samuel 1, verses 5 to 8; Isaiah 53, verses 7 to 12; 1 Corinthians 1, verses 26 to 29).

(c) *Psalm 147* falls into three sections with both the summons to praise and a reason repeated in each. The summonses occur in verses 1, 7 and 12.

Take note of the reasons for praise given in the sections following each summons. How do these reasons compare with the reasons noted in other psalms of praise you have read?

Discussion questions

Talking it through

1 To what degree are music and dance part of the praise of God in your community? If they are, how do they work for you? If not, do you wish they were?

2 Are there times in your own life when you feel you want to praise God without words? What are they? Are there other parts of your life or experience that could be considered 'praise' if you thought about it?

3 In the vein of Psalm 150, can you think of other ways in which creatures or inanimate objects in this world participate in the praise of God? Compare Psalm 148.

(a) If you were to create a banner for worship, what verse in Psalm 148 would you choose to illustrate? Why?

(b) In the cacophony of religious options today, is God's name 'alone' exalted (verse 13)?

Widening our horizons

1 Think together about the content of your
prayer, both corporately and personally.
(a) In your prayers of praise to God, what
reasons for praise are there?
(a) Do most of your prayers praise God for
what he has done for you or for *who*
God is? Which is harder to do? Why?
(b) Do you think you should alter the
balance? If so, how?

2 Does the praise in your community's
worship relate to your daily experience and
life, or does it tend to be all rather remote?
In what ways would you like to emulate the
psalmists? What themes appeal to you?

3 Is it possible to praise God too much, too
quickly or too easily? At what point does
praise become shallow?

4 Has the church generally lost the knowledge or
ability to praise God, or just the desire to do so?
Why is praise 'inner health made audible'?

Cultivating the practice of prayer

Praise the Lord!
How good it is to sing praises to our God;
for he is gracious, and a song of praise
is fitting.

Psalm 147, verse 1

Make Psalm 147 the basis of your prayer.

Read verses 1 to 6. Consider ways in
which God has healed the brokenhearted
and lifted the downtrodden. Give praise to
God for his work with other people. Pray
for those who are still brokenhearted and
seek God's healing for them.

Read verses 7 to 11. Consider the gracious
bounty of the Lord in creation. Give praise
to God who has made and provides for his
creatures. Pray that God may provide for
those people and creatures who do not at
present share that provision.

Read verses 12 to 20. Consider the word of
the Lord by which he grants us peace and
by which he judges us. Pray for the desire

and ability to hear that word. Pray for
those — others or yourself — who do not
at present know the peace God promises.

Let everything that breathes
   praise the Lord!
   Praise the Lord!

Psalm 150, verse 6

Notes

Appendix

Psalms according to their types

Many scholars have attempted to classify the psalms according to their types. The results are often quite varied depending on the categories the scholar selects, how they are understood and what assumptions are made about the way the psalms were used in Israel. The content of many psalms also lends itself to more than one category. Therefore, an exact classification is not possible. The following analysis is intended only as a guide for those who want to continue praying with psalms and is based on the chapters in this book. Psalms that fit more than one category are listed in brackets ( ). Repeated psalms or parts of psalms are indicated by equals signs in brackets (=).

Another detailed analysis can be found on pp.235–242 of Bernhard Anderson, *Out of the Depths*. See the Bibliography for details.

Psalms of creation
  8, 33, 104, 148

Psalms of *torah*
  1, 19, 119

Psalms of history
  (66), 78, 105, 106, 114, 135, 136

Psalms of individual lament
  3, 4, 5, 7, 9–10, 13, 14(=53)
  17, 22, 25, 26, (27), 28, 31
  35, 39, (40), 41, 42–43, 53(=14), 54
  55, 56, 57, 59, 61, (63), 64
  69, 70(=40:13–17), 71, 77, 86, 88, 109
  120, 139, 140, 141, 142

Psalms of community lament
  12, 44, 58, 60, 74, 79, 80
  83, 85, (89), 90, 94, (108), 123
  125, 126, 129, 137

Psalms of confession
  6, 32, 38, 51, 102, 130, 143

Psalms of trust and thanksgiving
  11, 16, 23, (27), 30, 34, (40)
  52, 62, (63), 65, (66), 67, 75
  91, 92, 107, 116, 118, 121, 124
  131, 138

Psalms of enthronement and royal psalms
    2, 18, 20, 21, (24), 45, 47
    72, (89), 93, 96, 97, 98, 99
    101, 110, 132, 144

Psalms of praise
    29, 95, 100, 103, (108), 111, 113
    117, 145, 147, 149, 150

Other hymns
Liturgies:	15, (24), 50, 81, 82, 115, 134
Wisdom Psalms:	37, 49, 73, 112, 127, 128, 133
Songs of Zion:	46, 48, 76, 84, 87, 122
Mixed type:	36, 68

Endnotes

Introduction

1. John Calvin, *Calvin's Commentaries*, Edinburgh, 1847, Vol. I, p.xxxviii
2. Martin Luther, *Word and Sacrament I*, Vol. 35 of *Luther's Works*, Philadelphia, 1960, p.256
3. Psalms 86, 101, 103, 108 to 110, 122, 124 and 131
4. Psalms 42 to 49, 84, 85, 87 and 88
5. Psalms 50, and 73 to 83
6. For a very detailed discussion of these psalm titles see Hans-Joachim Kraus, *Psalms 1–59*, Augsburg, 1988, pp.21–32
7. These are Psalms 3, 7, 18, 34, 51, 52, 54, 56, 57, 59, 60, 63 and 142. In the Hebrew text of these psalms, the headings are included in the first verse(s) of the text of the psalm. In most of our English Bibles (for example, NRSV, NJB, REB etc.) they are printed as separate headings, often in italics or small print. Editions of the GNB include the Hebrew title in a footnote. Only the NJV and the NAB follow the Hebrew text and its versification.
8. For further discussion, see Peter Craigie, *Psalms 1–50*, Word, 1983, pp.33–34
9. *Ibid*, pp.34–35

10. On the other hand, one cannot rule out the possibility of some psalms going back to David's time, if not to David himself. An example is most of Psalm 132. For more on this, see F.M. Cross, *Canaanite Myth and Hebrew Epic*, Harvard University, 1973, pp.94–97, 232–235

11. These are Psalm 18, verse 50; Psalm 78, verse 70; Psalm 89, verses 3, 20, 35 and 49; Psalm 132, verses 1, 10 to 12, 17; Psalm 144, verse 10 (compare Psalm 122, verse 5).

12. Even as early as the 2nd century BC, David would seem to be accredited as the psalmist if that is how we are to read Ecclesiasticus 47, verses 8 to 10.

13. A.M. Cooper, 'The Life and Times of King David according to the Books of Psalms', in *The Poet and the Historian: Essays in Literary and Historical Criticism*, Richard Friedman (ed.), Scholars Press, 1983, p.125

14. Brevard Childs, *Introduction to the Old Testament as Scripture*, Fortress, 1979, p.521

15. *Ibid*

16. A list of these quotations or allusions can be found in several basic texts of the psalms, including Leopold Sabourin, *The Psalms: Their Origin and Meaning*, Alba House, 1974, pp.164–170, and Bernhard Anderson, *Out of the Depths: The Psalms Speak for Us Today*, Westminster, 1983, pp.243–245

17. Romans 3, verse 4 (Psalm 51, verse 4; Psalm 116, verse 11); verses 10–12 (Psalm 14, verses 1 to 3); verse 13 (Psalm 140, verse 3); verse 13 (Psalm 5, verse 9); verse 14 (Psalm 10, verse 7) and verse 18 (Psalm 36, verse 1)

18. Psalm 22, verse 1 in Matthew 27, verse 46 and Mark 15, verse 34; Psalm 22, verse 7 in Matthew 27, verse 39 and Mark 15, verse 29; Psalm 22, verse 8 in Matthew 27, verse 43; Psalm 22, verse 18 in John 19, verse 24; and Psalm 22, verse 22 in Hebrews 2, verse 12

19. See Leslie Allen, *Psalms*, Word, 1987, p.126

20. Gunkel's small English volume, *The Psalms*, Fortress, 1967, is a translation of a 1930 encyclopaedia article.

21. For example, Gerald Wilson, *The Editing of the Hebrew Psalter*, Scholars Press, 1985

22. Patrick Miller, *Interpreting the Psalms*, Fortress, 1986, p.8

23. *Ibid*, p.22

24. Walter Brueggemann, *The Message of the Psalms*, Augsburg, 1984, p.17

25. *Ibid*, pp.15–25

26. Peter Craigie, *Psalms 1–50*, Word, 1983, p.36

Chapter 1

1. Walter Brueggemann, *The Message of the Psalms*, Augsburg, 1984, p.26

2. A translation of this myth can be found in *Ancient Near Eastern Texts Relating to the Old Testament*, James Pritchard (ed.), 3rd. ed., Princeton University Press, 1969, pp.60 to 72.

3. Claus Westermann, *The Living Psalms*, T.&T. Clark, 1989, p.207

4. The reference to a 'bottle' follows the ancient Greek translation whereas the Hebrew text reads 'like a heap'.

5. For example, Peter Craigie, *Psalms 1–50*, Word, 1983, p.271

6. The word 'warrior' is a parallel term to 'king'.

7. Peter Craigie, *op.cit.*, p.275

8. This phrase is also found in Psalm 40, verse 3; Psalm 96, verse 1; Psalm 98, verse 1; Psalm 149, verse 1; Isaiah 42, verse 10; etc.

9. Note that Revelation 5, verse 9 uses the term 'new song' to speak about the song to be sung at the culmination of God's reign.

10. Peter Craigie, *op.cit.*, p.272

Chapter 2

1. The ancient Hittite empire was centred on modern-day Turkey and the Hittite law codes date to the fourteenth century BC.

2. Richard Clifford, *Deuteronomy, with an Excursus on Covenant and Law*, Michael Glazier, 1982, p.187

3. Walter Brueggemann, *The Message of the Psalms*, Augsburg, 1984, p.38

4. C.S. Lewis, *Reflections on the Psalms*, Geoffrey Bles, 1958, p.56

5. For example Artur Weiser, *The Psalms*, SCM, 1962, pp.197–204

6. For example, the Egyptian hymns to the sun-god Aten, the text of which can be found in *Ancient Near Eastern Texts Relating to the Old Testament*, James Pritchard (ed.), Princeton University Press, 1969, pp. 369–371

7. The same effect is achieved to a much greater extent in Psalm 119 where each eight-verse section repeats roughly the same set of synonyms. The total effect of all 176 verses is to focus our attention on the *torah* of the Lord.

8. See for example on this, J.T. Glass, 'Some Observations on Psalm 19', in *The Listening Heart: Essays in Wisdom and Psalms in Honor of Roland E. Murphy*, K.G. Hoglund et al (eds.), JSOT Press, 1987, pp.147–160, esp. p.149

9. Michael Fishbane, *Text and Texture: Close Readings of Selected Biblical Texts*, Schocken, 1979, p.88

10. *Ibid*, p.90

Chapter 3

1. While Psalm 106, verse 1 is a verse found frequently throughout the Book of Psalms and verse 48 is a doxology at the end of Book 4 of the Book of Psalms bearing similarities to the doxologies at the end of Books 1 to 3,

it is clear from the quotation, especially of verse 47 in 1 Chronicles 16, verse 35, that Psalm 106 is being used.

2. Note that 1 Chronicles 16, verses 8 to 22 is Psalm 105, verses 1 to 15 and verses 23 to 33 is Psalm 96, verses 1 to 12a with small variations.

3. Compare, for example, Psalm 107, verse 1; Psalm 118, verses 1 and 29; Psalm 136, verses 1 to 3, 26, etc.

4. Brevard S. Childs, *Memory and Tradition in Israel*, SCM, 1962, p.42

5. See also C. Hyde, 'The Rememberance of the Exodus in the Psalms', *Worship 52* (1988), p.410

6. Leslie C. Allen, *Psalms 101–150*, Word, 1983, p.55

Chapter 4

1. Walter Brueggemann, 'From Hurt to Joy, Death to Life', *Interpretation 28*, 1974, pp.3–19

2. *Ibid*, p.5

3. For example, Jeremiah 11 to 20, Lamentations 3, Jonah 2

4. Bernhard Anderson, *Out of the Depths*, Westminster, 1983, pp.76–77

5. See Walter Brueggemann, 'The Formfulness of Grief', *Interpretation 31*, 1977, pp.263–275 or 'The Costly Loss of Lament', *Journal for the Study of the Old Testament 36*, 1986, pp.57–71

6. Sigmund Mowinckel, *The Psalms in Israel's Worship*, Blackwell, 1962, Vol.II, pp.58–61

7. This argument is based on the salvation oracles of the prophets — for example, Jeremiah 30, verses 10 and 11; Isaiah, 41, verses 8 to 13; and Isaiah 43, verses 1 to 7. Although note that four psalms actually have the Lord's answer to the petition — namely, Psalm 12, verse 5; Psalm 60, verse 6; Psalm 91, verses 15 and 16; and Psalm 108, verse 7. This answer was possibly spoken by a priest as part of the liturgy.

8. C.C. Broyles, *The Conflict of Faith and Experience in the Psalms*, Sheffield Academic Press, 1989, pp.185–187. Claus Westermann, *Praise and Lament in the Psalms*, John Knox, 1981, pp.70ff., also argues that the change from petition to praise indicates that such psalms already hold within them an element of trust or turning to the Lord — for example, Psalm 13, verse 5, and Psalm 22, verse 22.

9. C.C. Broyles, *op.cit.*, pp.51–53

10. *Ibid*, pp.52–53

11. S.J.L. Croft, *The Identity of the Individual in the Psalms*, JSOT Press, 1987, pp.67–72

12. Patrick Miller, 'Trouble and Woe: Interpreting Biblical Laments', *Interpretation 37*, 1983, pp.32–45, especially p.35

13. Ellen Davis, 'Exploding the Limits: Form and Function in Psalm 22', *Journal for the Study of the Old Testament*, 53 (1992) pp.93–105, especially p.96

14. Ellen Davis notes that elsewhere in the Book of Psalms the dead are said not to be able to praise God. Rather than seeing an understanding of a doctrine of resurrection in the psalm, which would date the psalm exceptionally late, she concludes 'that the present invocation of the dead is much better explained in terms of the poet's extravagance of expression than in terms of the more sober development of religious dogma [about the resurrection]', *ibid*, pp.102–103

15. Patrick Miller, *Interpreting The Psalms*, Fortress, 986, p.109

16. *Ibid*, p.110

17. C.S. Lewis, *Reflections on the Psalms*, Geoffrey Bles, 1958, p.20

Chapter 5

1. For example Sigmund Mowinckel, *The Psalms in Israel's Worship*, Blackwell, 1962

2. Peter Craigie, *Psalms 1–50*, Word Books, 1983, p.332
3. *Ibid*, p.331 where Craigie suggests the singular might indicate the king speaking and sees a clear structure in the psalm based on the speaker.
4. *Ibid*, p.335
5. J.F. Craghan, *The Psalms: Prayers for the Ups, Downs and In-Betweens of Life*, Michael Glazier, 1986, p.144
6. Richard Clifford, 'Psalm 89: A Lament over the Davidic Ruler's Continued Failure,' *Harvard Theological Review*, 73, 1980, pp.35ff

Chapter 6

1. Martin Luther, 'The Seven Penitential Psalms', *Luther's Works*, Jeroslav Pelikan (ed.), Concordia, 1958, Vol.14, pp.140–205
2. See Leopold Sabourin, *The Psalms: Their Origin and Meaning*, Alba House, 1974, p.241 for more on the origin of this title.
3. These words are based on the same Hebrew root word, i.e. the word for 'face'.
4. The metaphor of washing is used also in Isaiah 1, verse 16 and Jeremiah 4, verse 14.
5. Note that Claus Westermann makes a similar point and reminds us that sin in the Old Testament is never thought of as some permanent state in which we live from birth, but rather as 'something which is done' (*The Living Psalms*, T.&T. Clark, 1989, p.96).
6. The view that all sin is against God is shared by other Old Testament passages — for example, Genesis 39, verse 9 and 2 Samuel chapter 12, verse 13.
7. Walter Brueggemann, *The Message of the Psalms*, Augsburg, 1984, p.99
8. Note that the Hebrew is uncertain as to precisely where

such truth is found.

9. Compare Psalm 104, verses 28 to 30
10. Claus Westermann, *op. cit.*, pp.100–101

Chapter 7

1. The close connection between psalms of lament and psalms of praise can be seen in the fact that the vow of praise at the end of a lament can be the same as the statement at the beginning of praise. For example, compare Psalm 56, verse 13 with Psalm 30, verse 1.

2. Peter Craigie, *Psalms 1–50*, Word, 1983, pp.204–205, although he notes that the division is debated.

3. The shepherd metaphor of verses 1 to 3 need not necessarily be continued in verse 4, nor does verse 6 necessarily continue the metaphor of the banquet from verse 5. Moreover, verse 3 concludes with a reason for the statements in verses 1 to 3, and verse 6 begins with an initial particle in Hebrew, indicating an independent statement.

4. Patrick Miller, *Interpreting the Psalms*, Fortress, 1986, p.115

5. *Ancient Near Eastern Texts Relating to the Old Testament*, James Pritchard (ed.), Princeton, 1969, p.387

6. *Ibid*, p.443

7. Compare Isaiah 11, verses 6 and 7 for an image of animals lying down together as a symbol of security.

8. See, for example, 1 Samuel 12, verse 22; Psalm 79, verse 9; Psalm 106, verse 8; Psalm 109, verse 21; Psalm 143, verse 11; Jeremiah 14, verse 21; Ezekiel 20, verse 9.

9. See the NRSV with its footnote for these variations in translation.

10. See *The Amarna Letters*, W.L. Moran (ed.), Johns Hopkins University, 1992, pp.172–173

11. David Freedman, 'The Twenty Third Psalm', in *Michigan Oriental Studies in Honor of George C. Cameron*, L.I. Orlin

(ed.), University of Michigan, 1976, p.160

12. Artur Weiser, *The Psalms*, SCM, 1962, p.227
13. *Ibid*
14. *Ibid*,p.228
15. Claus Westermann, *The Living Psalms*, T.&T. Clark, 1989, p.131. Also compare Hans-Joachim Kraus, *Psalms 1–59*, Augsburg, 1988, p.309
16. Claus Westermann, *op. cit.*, p.132
17. Artur Weiser, *op. cit.*, p.777

Chapter 8

1. This poem could date, according to some scholars, to the mid-twelfth century BC, over a century before Saul and David come on the scene.
2. See 1 Samuel 8 to 12, where the struggle over human and divine kingship is evident.
3. Walter Brueggemann, *The Message of the Psalms*, Augsburg, 1984, p.151. Compare Leviticus 25, verse 42.
4. For details of Mowinckel's view see Sigmund Mowinckel, *The Psalms in Israel's Worship*, Blackwell, 1962, Vol.1, pp.106–192.
5. For a description of the *akitu* festival, see *Ancient Near Eastern Texts Relating to the Old Testament*, James Pritchard (ed.), Princeton University Press, 1969, p.342.
6. For one description of the Festival of Booths, see Deuteronomy 16, verses 13 to 15.
7. See S.J.L. Croft, *The Identity of the Individual in the Psalms*, JSOT Press, 1987, pp.81–84, for a description of the proposed festival.
8. It is clear that the people are addressed in verse 5 as plural verb forms are used.
9. For a description of what the earthly king was ideally expected to do, see Psalm 72 below.

Chapter 9

1. Patrick Miller, *Interpreting the Psalms*, Fortress, 1986, p.64
2. Claus Westermann, *Praise and Lament in the Psalms*, John Knox, 1981, p.122
3. C.C. Broyles, *The Conflict of Faith and Experience in the Psalms*, Sheffield Academic Press, 1989, pp.51–53
4. For example, Claus Westermann, *op.cit.*, pp.250–258 and Patrick Miller, *op.cit.*, p.67
5. *Ibid*, p.67
6. *Ibid*,p.68
7. Claus Westermann, *op.cit.*, p.31
8. Walter Brueggemann, *Israel's Praise: Doxology against Idolatry and Ideology*, Fortress, 1988, p.11
9. *Ibid*,p.155
10. Leslie Allen, *Psalms 100–150*, Word, 1983, p.324

Bibliography

Useful commentaries on Psalms

Walter Brueggemann, *The Message of the Psalms*, Augsburg, 1984

An excellent one-volume commentary. It gives reasonably brief comments on about one-third of the psalms.

Peter Craigie, *Psalms 1–50*, Word, 1983
Marvin Tate, *Psalms 51–100*, Word, 1990
Leslie Allen, *Psalms 101–150*, Word, 1983

An excellent series of technical commentaries with a good range of current opinion and bibliography on each psalm.

Hans-Joachim Kraus, *Psalms 1–59: A Commentary*, Augsburg, 1988
Hans-Joachim Kraus, *Psalms 60–150: A Commentary*, Augsburg, 1989

A highly technical series, but with excellent theological comments for those interested in this type of commentary.

Carroll Stuhlmueller, *Psalms*, 2 vols, Michael Glazier, 1983

A good introductory commentary on historical critical lines.

Artur Weiser, *The Psalms*, SCM, 1962

The most exhaustive one-volume technical commentary available, but a little dated now.

Claus Westermann, *The Living Psalms*, T.&T. Clark, 1989
A good one-volume commentary covering most psalms. Non-technical in language.

Useful investigations of key ideas in Psalms
❏ *Introductions*

Peter Ackroyd, *Doors of Perception: A Guide to Reading the Psalms*, SCM, 1983
A good brief introduction to the types of psalms, their background and poetry.

Leslie Allen, *Psalms*, Word, 1987
A readable introduction to the whole Book of Psalms.

Bernhard Anderson, *Out of the Depths*, Westminster, rev. ed., 1983
A very useful introduction to the types of psalms and their background.

Patrick Miller, *Interpreting the Psalms*, Fortress, 1986
This is a collection of articles by Miller on how the Psalms have meaning well beyond their original context. Ten psalms are dealt with in detail.

Leopold Sabourin, *The Psalms: Their Origin and Meaning*, Alba House, 1970
A detailed introduction to issues relating to the psalms, with brief commentary on all psalms. In spite of its date, a useful book for those seeking a detailed introduction.

Klaus Seybold, *Introducing the Psalms*, T.&T. Clark, 1990
An excellent introduction to types of psalms and other technical matters, but also with an interest in the history of psalm collection and interpretation.

Mark Smith, *Psalms: The Divine Journey*, Paulist, 1987

A lively introduction to theological issues relating to the whole collection of Psalms.

Claus Westermann, *The Psalms: Structure, Content and Message*, Augsburg, 1980

A general introduction to the canonical Book of Psalms.

❏ *Technical matters*

Hermann Gunkel, *The Psalms: A Form-Critical Introduction*, Fortress, 1967

A translation of a 1930 encyclopaedia article that has proved groundbreaking for modern Psalms study.

Othmar Keel, *The Symbolism of the Biblical World: Ancient Near Eastern Iconography and the Book of Psalms*, Seabury, 1978

A large collection of pictures and drawings of various reliefs, paintings, sculptures and other artifacts that have been found by archaeologists and which are informative for understanding the imagery and background of the Psalms.

Hans-Joachim Kraus, *Theology of the Psalms*, Augsburg, 1986

A scholarly summation of the theology found in the Book of Psalms. It has much useful material for those interested in a highly technical approach.

Sigmund Mowinckel, *The Psalms in Israel's Worship*, Blackwell, 1962

Another major classic of modern Psalms study. Highly technical.

H.H. Rowley, 'Psalmody and Music', *Worship in Ancient Israel*, SPCK, 1967, pp.176–212

A useful study of music and psalms in ancient Israel.

The journal *Interpretation* occasionally has a series of articles on various aspects of the Psalms with some brief expository articles, as well as readable theological and technical ones — for example, volumes 28/1 (1974), 39/1 (1985) and 46/2 (1992).

Useful treatment of present-day faith and life issues raised in Psalms

❑ *Prayer and worship*

Walter Brueggemann, *Israel's Praise: Doxology against Idolatry and Ideology*, Fortress, 1988
A thought-provoking work on the psalms of praise and how they can both reflect and shape our thinking about God.

Walter Brueggemann, *Praying the Psalms*, Saint Mary's, 1982
A evocative series of essays on how Christians could use the psalms more honestly and creatively.

Dietrich Bonhoeffer, *Psalms: The Prayer Book of the Bible*, Augsburg, 1970
A very brief series of comments on different types of psalms from one of the foremost Christian theologians of the twentieth century. Thought provoking.

J.F. Craghan, *The Psalms: Prayers for the Ups, Downs and In-Betweens of Life*, Michael Glazier, 1988
A general introduction with reference to the relation of psalms to the lives of those who use them.

T. Craven, *The Books of Psalms*, Liturgical Press, 1992
A handy introduction to the language of the psalms and how they contribute to Christian spirituality.

G.S. Dawson, 'Praying the Difficult Psalms', *Weavings* 6/5 (1991), pp.28–35

Addresses the difficult question of how to pray the psalms which speak of revenge on the enemy. It offers some useful solutions.

E.S. Gerstenberger, 'Enemies and evildoers in the Psalms: A Challenge to Christian Preaching', *Horizons in Biblical Theology*, 4/5 (1982–83), pp.61–77

Argues against the avoidance of the questions of who are the 'enemies' in the psalms and in our contemporary world. Confronting such questions ought to be a subject of Christian preaching.

W.L. Holladay, *The Psalms through Three Thousand Years: Prayerbook of a Cloud of Witnesses*, Fortress, 1993

A readable, comprehensive study of the Book of Psalms, it shows ways the Psalms have been used in Christian worship through the centuries — and some theological issues arising from a study of psalms.

M. Israel, *A Light on the Path: An Exploration of Integrity through the Psalms*, DLT, 1990

A useful book addressing questions of personal integrity and spiritual development in relation to the psalms.

C.S. Lewis, *Reflections on the Psalms*, Geoffrey Bles, 1958

This is an older book on general topics to do with the Psalms by a popular Christian writer. It has much that is still of use and interest to the Christian reader.

R.E. Prothero, *The Psalms in Human Life*, John Murray, 1904

This older work is a rich collection of examples and stories of how the Psalms have been used in the Christian church from its earliest days until the beginnings of the twentieth century.

M.H. Shepherd, *The Psalms in Christian Worship: A Practical Guide*, Augsburg, 1976

This is a readable summary of how the Psalms have been used throughout christian history.

The journal *Reformed Liturgy and Worship* sometimes has collections of articles on the psalms and worship — for example, volume xxiii/i (1989).

Music
There are many new books giving musical settings for the Psalms. I am not qualified to comment on them. A good theological library should be able to introduce you to many of them.

The journal *Reformed Liturgy and Worship* sometimes has collections of articles on the psalms and music — for example, volume xiv/4 (1980) on singing the psalms.

Index to Psalms
referred to in this book

The psalm numbers are in **bold**. The page numbers which refer to the various psalms are in *italics*.

Notes

Notes